THE LITTLE GUIDE TO
Your
Well-Read Life

THE LITTLE GUIDE TO
Your
Well-Read Life

*How to get more books in your life
and more life from your books*

STEVE
LEVEEN

LEVENGER
PRESS

Published by
Levenger Press
420 South Congress Avenue
Delray Beach, Florida 33445-4696 USA
www.Levengerpress.com 800.544.0880

For permission to quote from this material, contact the Editor of
Levenger Press at the above address.

Library of Congress Cataloging-in-Publication Data

Leveen, Steve, 1954-
  The little guide to your well-read life / Steve Leveen.
      p. cm.
  Includes bibliographical references and index.
  ISBN 1-929154-17-8 (hardcover, illustrated)
  1. Books and reading. I. Title.
Z1003.L544 2005
028'.9--dc22
                                    2004013918

Library of Congress Control Number: 2004115530

Cover and book design by Danielle Furci, Levenger Studios
Lee Passarella, Creative Director

Printed in the United States of America by RR Donnelley

Mission
To create and sell meaningful products for the productive
enjoyment of reading, writing, and working with ideas

For my mother, Ada

Read in order to Live.

—Gustave Flaubert

Contents

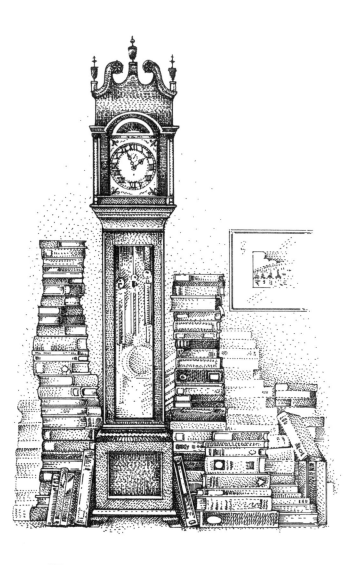

*B*ook-love...*never flags or fails, but, like*
Beauty itself, is a joy for ever.

—Holbrook Jackson

Book Love Regained

Do you wish you had more time to read? This little guide can help you make that wish come true.

It is a book for readers who want more in their lives. It will show you how to do a better job finding books you'll love, how to read more of them, how to retain more from them—and as a result, how to live a larger life.

A different kind of reading tool

When my wife, Lori, and I founded Levenger and started selling "tools for serious readers," our customers graciously purchased our reading lights, bookcases, and notebooks. Yet there was one repeated request we could not fulfill. Again and again customers said to us, "What I really need is more time to read. I just wish you could give me *that*."

As a merchant, I found it frustrating to hear customers express such a deep desire and not be able to satisfy it.

But then I met a fellow who made it his hobby to ask people about their favorite books in order to build his own ideal reading list. I learned about people who fill their libraries with hundreds of carefully chosen books they would really like to read. I discovered readers who read lots of books by listening to them. I encountered people who praised their reading groups for how much more they gained from books shared this way.

Other readers described how they retained more from their books if they wrote in the margins or made summaries in note-books. Still others became born-again readers due to some signal event (often a personal setback) and expressed how grateful they were for their rebirth.

I began to wonder if I should collect these techniques and stories to share with our customers. If I couldn't literally give them more time, perhaps I could give them tools for getting more books into the time they had.

A second, even more personal reason drove me to attempt this task: my own strong feeling that it was finally time—in my middle years—to repair my own ill-read life.

Late to the bookshelf

Growing up, I was not one of those precocious children who began reading serious books at a young age. What's more, I never became much of a reader in school. A couple of books in high school caught my interest, and a few more in college and graduate school, but I'm embarrassed to admit that most of the books my well-meaning instructors assigned went forlornly unread. The list of books I was *supposed* to read is impressive: *The Iliad* and *The Odyssey*, *The Oxford New Testament*, numerous Shakespearean plays and sonnets, *The Decameron*, *Don Quixote*, *Moby-Dick*, *A Separate Peace*, and so on and on. Virtually any list of important classics would have precious few check marks from me. Somehow, with Cliffs Notes and cunning, I faked my way through.

Not that I didn't taste the sweetness of book enlightenment. In college, I actually did read Voltaire's short and approachable *Candide*, and it had a marked impact on me. (I then saw the Leonard Bernstein musical three times.) In grad school, Leo Marx's *Machine in the Garden* opened my eyes to the reservations

I felt about technology. I learned that rather than being new to our age, my concerns were as old as the Roman hills. And after reading R. Murray Schafer's *The Tuning of the World*, my ears were opened, never to hear the world the same way again.

Later, in my thirties, Stanley Marcus's *Minding the Store* came into my hands at the right time and showed me my calling as a merchant. These books were potent elixirs and gave me a thirst for more.

Yet I suppressed that thirst. Like so many young people beginning their careers, I had my nose to one grindstone after another, missing—as my young adulthood loped by—great books in all their varieties. I nodded to them in passing, like a busy neighbor. I knew some of their names, but I was living in their shadow rather than taking them into my life and running on their fuel.

So it was also midlife pangs of missed opportunity that drove me to this task. What useful advice I hoped to offer others, I thirsted for myself. I wanted, intensely, to get more life into the rest of my life.

While I spent two years writing this book, on reflection I realize that I have actually been working on it for about twelve years. That was when I began listening to unabridged audiobooks, an experience that changed my life. I was reborn to a life of reading, and therein began a process whose momentum is still building. In the past twelve months, I've read more books (with my ears and eyes) than in any other year of my life. As a result, my life has become electrified and zestful—like living in color rather than black and white.

Making up for lost time

Seeing how my life was becoming so much fuller fired my ambition to find other ways people got back into reading as adults. I began to interview people from different professions whom I knew to be serious readers, including attorneys, scientists, librarians, physicians, scholars, writers, book reviewers, editors, and businesspeople. Usually I traveled to their offices with my laptop and tape recorder and interrogated them with all manner of questions about how they selected their books, how they read, when they read, whether speed reading courses had ever helped, how they sought to retain what they had read, and so forth. Frequently I tested the patience of busy people, yet by and large they were enthusiastic, if somewhat bemused, as they tried to answer questions they had never before considered.

In addition to these interviews, I found a heritage of works devoted to the phenomenon of reading—books such as James Baldwin's *Book-Lover* (1885), Holbrook Jackson's *The Reading of Books* (1947), and Harold Bloom's *How to Read and Why* (2000). These and others offered wide-ranging insights into what reading is all about and how it can transform lives.

Finally, I sought out biographies. How did some great achievers, such as John Adams and Nelson Mandela, manage to become impassioned readers and lead such remarkably active lives?

Gradually I began to see that there were practical techniques people have found to get more books into their lives. Men and women did manage to enrich themselves with the written wisdom and wit of humankind, despite the pressing demands and urgent trivialities that plague the human race.

What I found often surprised me.

Dispelling a few myths

I was surprised that many of the classic books we've heard about are not difficult and ponderous but instead, readable and fascinating. Though you sometimes encounter lengthy introductions better read afterward, you can easily jump over these moats and walk in the castle door, often to find a friendly dwelling you will thereafter consider your own.

On the other hand, there are also classics and important works that aren't a bit useful or good—some not good for me and others not good for you. No classic exists that *everyone* loves and admires. Moreover, it is liberating to accept this and care not a whit when some treasured classic isn't treasure for you.

I was pleasantly surprised that many widely read people are not bookish stereotypes but vigorous actors on the stage of life. While there are some retiring booklovers who don't engage the real world, there are plenty who engage books and life with equal passion. Read about Theodore Roosevelt, Douglas MacArthur, Winston Churchill, T. E. Lawrence, and that 1930s African bush pilot and writer named Beryl Markham to see how living a life of the mind and a life of action can reinforce each other. Reading books that excite and teach you can lead to experiences you would not have had. These experiences, in turn, lead to more books you would not have uncovered. Many of the most engaged and interesting people in history seem to have been swept up into a whirling dance, laughing with life, one arm crooked into experience and the other into books.

Finally, I was surprised by what actually constituted a well-read life.

What does well-read really mean?

As Will Rogers observed, we all don't know something. No one can be well-read in all or even most things.

Not once in my interviews did I come across readers who described *themselves* as well-read. It seems to be a term we use to describe others, but not ourselves. This may be partly out of modesty, but it is mainly due, I think, to true insight. The more books you read, the more titles and topics you uncover. The more you know, the better you understand how little you really do know.

A large bookstore today can offer 100,000 titles. Major libraries preserve millions of volumes. And online, you can find over six million volumes in English. Compare these numbers with an active reading life of, say, fifty books a year or five hundred books a decade. It's natural to feel discouraged when we finally face the facts: there's a yawning expanse of delicious knowledge and captivating stories we are fated never to know.

No less a reader than Winston Churchill lamented this. "Think of all the wonderful tales that have been told, and well told, which you will never know. Think of all the searching inquiries into matters of great consequence which you will never pursue."

But don't let the numbers overwhelm you. Instead, think of how you respond to this simple question: "So…are you reading anything good these days?"

Being in book love

If you can answer along the lines of, "Oh yes! I'm reading this wonderful book now and I can't wait to get back to it; it's called so-and-so and it's about such-and-such," then you are in book love.

Any of us might live a long life or pass away tomorrow. I have come to believe that living your well-read life is measured not by the number of books read at the end of your life but by whether you are in book love today, tomorrow, and next week.

Book love is something like romantic love. When we are reading a really great book, burdens feel lighter, cares seem smaller, and commonplaces are suddenly delightful. You become your best optimistic self. Like romantic love, book love fills you with a certain warmth and completeness. The world holds promise. The atmosphere is clearer and brighter; a beckoning wind blows your hair.

But while romantic love can be fleeting, book love can last. Readers in book love become more skilled at choosing books that thrill them, move them, transport them. Success breeds success, as these lucky people learn how to find diamonds over and over. They are always reading a good book. They are curious, interested—and usually interesting—people. That keen observer of reading, Holbrook Jackson, wrote in 1931, "Book-love…never flags or fails, but, like Beauty itself, is *a joy for ever.*"

It's not only fiction that can produce book love. The right advice-filled book at the right time in your life can speak to you so vividly, it's as if the author were writing just to you. And great history, when it makes the past "as interesting as it actually was," as the historian David McCullough says, can grab a reader's imagination as powerfully as a novel. A book on virtually any subject, when written well and falling into the right hands, can produce a transcendent emotional response. And one such experience can lead to another and another, in a delightfully unpredictable way that is different for each person.

It is said that no love is sincerer than the love of food. Perhaps no love is vaster in its particulars than the love of books.

As adults, we can use the power of book love not only to entertain us, but also to inspire us to do new things, and to make significant changes in our lives. We can even use our love of books to help others, and maybe save a bit of the world.

That's what reading is all about—the pure pleasure of it, how it changes you, how you live your life differently because of what you read.

Your well-read life is yours alone

Your life is yours to discover and create, and few things are as important as for you to find those books that seem to have been written for you. Some, by good luck, will find you, but most—and certainly most of the truly great ones—you must seek out.

Do not set out to live *a* well-read life but rather *your* well-read life. No one can be well-read using someone else's reading list. Unless a book is good for you, you won't connect with it and gain from it. Just as no one can tell you how to lead your life, no one can tell you what to read for your life.

Living your well-read life is a way of living higher, with your eyes open to an astonishing world and your mind daily learning more—about the world, yourself, and your untapped capabilities.

Have you ever wished you had more time to read? You may as well wish you had more time to live. You do.

*Never force yourself to read a book that you do not enjoy.
There are so many good books in the world that it is foolish
to waste time on one that does not give you pleasure.*

—Atwood H. Townsend

1

Uncovering the Books That Will Change Your Life

Choosing books to read can seem an overwhelming task. Each week thousands of additional titles are added to the imponderable number already weighing down libraries and cramming bookstores.

Feeling oppressed by the number of books is nothing new. In the 1700s, Voltaire worried that "the multitude of books is making us ignorant." John Ruskin, the eminent English essayist and critic who died in 1900, complained of "these days of book deluge."

Yet most people I've talked to don't put a lot of time into developing a list of books they'd like to read. It's not something they plan, particularly. They may have a few books at home they intend to read—some they bought, some were gifts perhaps. It's usually kind of accidental and ad hoc.

So casual an approach is unfortunate when you think about how much a great book can mean. A single right book at the right time can change our views dramatically, give a quantum boost to our knowledge, help us to construct a whole new outlook on the world and our life. Isn't it odd that we don't seek those experiences more systematically?

What's more, when you read a book that deeply pleases you, it sets up a momentum. If it's the author who touched you, you then often seek out more of his or her books. If it's the topic, often the author will recommend further good reading, and you're off on a new adventure.

Conversely, an unfulfilling reading experience—say, of a book someone gave you—may dampen your enthusiasm, causing your reading to languish, sometimes for long periods.

While we have the freedom to have no plan, we also have the freedom *to* plan—to take control of our reading lives. For most people, this is a different way of thinking about books, and the results can be transforming.

The self-taught reader

It is said by wise teachers that the most important thing to learn in school is how to teach oneself—to learn how to learn. The embodiment of this concept is taking control over your own reading.

No matter how good a book may be judged by people in general, now or in years past, readers aren't general, they're particular. Books can be good only to the extent that a reader becomes involved in them. As Emerson said, "'Tis the good reader that makes the good book." And this happens one reader at a time. Only when you choose to read a book and are enthusiastic about it does it have a chance to be a good book for you.

Having a living list of books to read is a critical part of getting the most from your reading life, and it must be your *own* list, one you create. This cannot be left to someone else. Not only will your list be far more likely to please you, but much benefit lies in making the list. That is where your adventure begins.

Developing your List of Candidates

I like to call this list that you make for yourself a List of Candidates rather than a reading list. Most of us had assigned reading lists in school, and hence the term carries a tweed-jacketed pall of obligation. It is more helpful to consider the books you place on your list as *candidates for your attention* rather than obligations. Creating a List of Candidates engenders an open-ended, exploratory process rather than a closed, prescriptive solution.

Begin by choosing a method for keeping your list—a list that will grow and continuously evolve. It will not be a single list of books but rather, groupings of books under different headings. You will decide on the headings as you go along, adding more, deleting some, rearranging others.

Some people will prefer a paper journal, others an electronic one. Choose whatever is comfortable for you. It's the process of making and keeping the list that's important.

One easy way to start is with the authors or books you already know you want to read. Write them down under headings that make sense to you. Perhaps there are a few business or professional books you've been meaning to read, books about your next career, and books on places you plan to visit. Write these down. It is helpful to have access to an online bookseller (of new, used, and out-of-print books), where you can quickly check authors, titles, and subjects.

This list will also be where you write down the recommendations you receive from various sources. When you add these books, include a note on how you came to add them and when. Name the friend who recommended the book, the book review you read, or the movie you saw and then heard that the book was better. These comments will be helpful reminders in the future as you weigh the importance of various titles.

Looking back to go forward: your Bookography

Do you have a list of what you've already read? Most people I've talked to do not but wish they did. Part of this wish is purely pragmatic, in order to avoid buying or borrowing the same book again, but there is more to it. Such a list is like a diary, offering us perhaps even more insights into ourselves than the conventional kind. A list of books that meant something to you becomes a sort of book biography, or Bookography. Try to reconstruct such a list and you'll be in store for some rewarding self-knowledge.

It would probably be overwhelming to try to record every book that was important to you, so don't aim for completeness—just begin with any of the books you're *really glad you read*. List what you can remember of the title and author, and the approximate date when you read the book. The idea is to be exploratory—to look back at your reading for clues to what you'll most enjoy as you go forward. Your Bookography becomes an important way of adding new titles to your List of Candidates.

As you list the books you've enjoyed, ask yourself why the book was important to you. Was it the author's style that you liked so much? If so, perhaps you'd like other books by that author. Make the author a heading in your List of Candidates. Was it the topic that meant so much? Make that a heading. Perhaps a classic you read in school touched you. The classics, too, can be a heading.

Digging deep into yourself

In making your List of Candidates, cast your net wide. Be liberal with categories and interests. If you are trying to advance in your career or evolve into a new one, these will lead to certain obvious categories, but look for the not-so-obvious categories, too. Listen to those whispers within you. Recall your youth. Was there a subject you didn't study but wanted to? What interests did you defer because they were not likely to lead to a job? Perhaps you will list musical theater or sports history. Or the botany of alpine meadows or the South Pacific of James Cook. Maybe you've always wanted to learn Greek philosophy or to read in Italian. Your interests are still there. What do you hear calling?

Write down your ideas and categories no matter how evanescent they appear in your mind's eye, and even if they aren't part of what you think your future will bring. If they seem unlikely, so much the better; your adventures will contain that many more surprises.

For most of your subjects, you won't know what the great books are that cover those areas. That's the idea. This is what it means to direct your reading actively rather than passively. You can now enjoy finding the best books in your areas of interest. In nearly every subject area conceivable, books have been written by remarkable souls with loving care. If you will find your books, they will flower in your hands. They were written for a reader like you.

Don't expect to come up with all your categories of interest in one sitting—or even many sittings. It can be hard mental work as you reflect and imagine and plan. Do expect your list to evolve and expand and become ever more valuable to you. Feel free to follow new paths without feeling any obligation to read the books. Remember, these are candidates.

You may find as you create your list that you are doing more than writing down your interests; you are also setting goals. For nearly every goal is supported by reading—from improving your professional life and learning a new skill to traveling and nurturing personal relationships. Your List of Candidates is not merely a guide to your future reading: it is a guide to your future.

Building your Library of Candidates

You probably already have some books at home that you plan to read. I suggest that you expand this to a whole new level: a to-read library in which you gradually accumulate shelves of books, in different categories, that you plan to read—a Library of Candidates that evolves from your list. Instead of having five books, have fifty, or a hundred, or more.

Once it has scale, your Library of Candidates can reward you with experience, education, and entertainment, while it grows to richer proportions. Italo Calvino, the acclaimed twentieth-century Italian novelist and champion of the classics, recommended that fully half the books in your library belong to the to-read section. What's more, he advised, "leave a section of empty spaces, for surprises, and chance discoveries."

As your Library of Candidates grows, you may want to label the shelves. Included in mine is a Modern Classics category. These are *my* ideas of modern classics. I currently have Viktor Frankl's *Man's Search for Meaning*, recounting his concentration camp insights. I have heard about this book often over the years, and read about it in Steven Covey's *Seven Habits of Highly Successful People*. And my friend Bob Beamon cited this book as having changed his viewpoint dramatically while in college. I have a couple of books by C. S. Lewis, since his name, too, keeps coming up. I have *The Lady in the Lake* by Raymond Chandler because my bookseller friend Rob Hittel told me that this was the book that transformed him into a booklover when just a young man. I have *Goodbye, Mister Chips* by James Hilton because I've come across the title so often, including in Michael Korda's history of the best-selling books of the twentieth century. And I have a book of short stories by Raymond Carver because I heard that he wrote them as well as Hemingway.

On another shelf marked Classics, I have a few self-chosen *old* classics. One is a two-volume Plutarch's *Lives.* The adventurous, charismatic author of two hundred westerns, Louis L'Amour, explained in his memoir how he made a lifelong practice of examining the personal libraries of learned people the world over; after the Bible, Plutarch's tome was the one he most frequently came across. I have Robert Fagle's new translations of *The Iliad* and *The Odyssey* because Jason Epstein, the editor and publisher, told me they were fabulous. (I may yet make amends for my college days.)

Since I love biographies, I have a long shelf devoted to them. I rejoice to see Edna St. Vincent Millay, Samuel Goldwyn, Katharine Graham, Walter Payton, and Sting waiting patiently for me to know them.

One of my favorite shelves is labeled For When I Go There. It holds books to read in particular places. *Arundel,* a 1929 novel by Kenneth Roberts that my mother-in-law, Evelyn Granger, recommended, is about the history of Maine. Next to it is *Touching My Father's Soul: A Sherpa's Journey to the Top of Everest,* by Jamling Tenzing Norgay, which my friend Rob Kennedy, who has climbed Everest, gave me. I will read this book immediately before my hoped-for trekking in Nepal. *Wind from the Carolinas* (about, surprisingly, the Bahamas), by Robert Wilder, came highly recommended by my good friend Chris Wheeler, who has frequently sailed Bahamian waters. And Les Standiford's novel, *Bone Key*, is waiting for me to devour over a long weekend down in the Florida Keys.

How even more vivid is *Lonesome Dove* by Larry McMurtry if you read it while sitting on a veranda looking out over a Texas landscape (as a friend has). How much more memorable is reading Pat Conroy's *Prince of Tides* while staying in a beach house in the Low Country of South Carolina (as I have). Just as writing down goals can have an almost magical effect on making them happen, having the books for the various places in the world you want to visit can help those trips come about, and sooner rather than later. Once there, your experiences and your reading will reinforce each other, creating memories more vivid than either could have alone.

I experienced this with Dava Sobel's *Longitude*, her svelte, captivating history of the Longitude Prize and how an ill-treated clock maker named John Harrison finally solved the scientific problem of his age. At the end of her book, she visits the Greenwich Time Museum in England and describes being just inches from the ticking clocks that John Harrison built in the 1700s. I was able to do the same thing, as is any visitor to the museum, and the experience was so much stronger because of her book. Likewise, the experience made her book all the more vivid in my memory. This is life energized by books.

Just recently I've delighted myself by learning a new skill from a specialized set of books. Being a boater, I had been frustrated by not being able to tie the right knot for an application. So I scoured bookstores and marine stores for the best books on knot tying.

Some had clear illustrations, while others added historical insights. Several referenced the mother-of-all-knot-books, the huge *Ashley Book of Knots*, which I also bought.

It was fun to read about the same knot, such as a rolling hitch used to tie fenders on a boat rail, in the various books. One, translated from Italian, exuded that country's proud heritage in sailing. Talk about hands-on history! I cherish my growing collection of knot books and the dozen or so knots I can now tie with confidence.

Also in my Library of Candidates is a collection of books I bought online on growing tomatoes. I have not yet taken the time to peruse them, but I smile when thinking of my much-anticipated first step into gardening.

What are your categories? Fill them with books you'd like to read and start gaining the satisfaction of knowing you have a pantry full of good food for your mind and spirit.

Should you borrow or buy?

The relationship between your List of Candidates and your Library of Candidates is a fluid one. You may choose to borrow from the public library many books on your List of Candidates, read them, record them in your Bookography, yet never own them. Other times, you may buy books for your Library of Candidates without having written them down first. Your list and your library will share categories. If John Steinbeck or Patagonia explorations is on your List of Candidates as a heading, it will eventually be a section of your Library of Candidates, too.

Will you read all the books on your list, or even in your library? Definitely not, and put no such obligation on yourself.

What's important is that you take charge of your reading life and radically increase the quality of the books in the pool that you select from.

Winston Churchill understood the bittersweet benefit of owning more good books than you'll be able to read. "If they cannot be your friends," he wrote, "let them at any rate be your acquaintances. If they cannot enter the circle of your life, do not deny them at least a nod of recognition."

Owning books has many advantages over just having them on your list. When a book is there waiting for you, you have the freedom to seize and enjoy it at any time. Norman Lewis, the author of the college text *How to Read Better and Faster*, exhorts readers to get books into their homes. "You will be surprised what psychological motivation there is in your having *physical possession* of the books you plan to read," he says.

Happily, owning your promising candidate books is easier now than at any time previously. If you can't find the books you're looking for in your neighborhood bookstore, you almost certainly can find them online, second-hand, and often quite inexpensively, even in hardcover. The ready access to millions of previously hard-to-find books is one of the blessings of our age.

Hold again the books that once held you

You may find it rewarding to acquire copies of books that held your fascination in earlier years—even all the way back to childhood.

I went online to buy another copy of my college freshman psychology text some thirty years later. What memories it brought back to see the old illustrations and experience even the familiar smell of the book again, not to mention recalling some of the material.

Holding these books again can rekindle old interests. You may want to delve deeper into an area of interest or track down other works by a favorite author of the time. Who knows where these reconnections may lead?

Recently I tracked down a 1935 edition of *Seven League Boots* by Richard Halliburton for my friend Elliot Goldstein. He'd mentioned how it had electrified him, while a boy, with intense wanderlust. Now in his late seventies, Elliot had done a good job of seeing the world. I'll never forget the appreciation in his voice when he called to thank me for reuniting him with his old friend. He had already begun reading it and knew he would fall in love with it once again.

Iffy advice from friends

Some of our best books come from friends who know us well and know the kinds of books we like. Yet most of us have had a friend rave about a book, only to find our own opinion almost entirely the opposite.

Having been let down a few times, I've since learned to ask friends *why* they liked the book so much. If you don't know each other all that well, it's probably best to note their recommendations on your List of Candidates and wait. Perhaps you'll come across another friend who recommends it, or you'll have the chance to examine it at a library or bookstore. The international Global Positioning System takes three satellites to fix a position and four satellites to fix it well. We might apply a similar concept to books that friends recommend.

Golden advice from acquaintances

One of the blessings of keeping your List of Candidates is that it can make your encounters and travels more interesting.

Let's say one of your interests is gardening, but you don't have much time for tending a garden at this stage in your life. Make it a heading on your List of Candidates and collect titles of recommended books. At least you have time for *that* now.

Then, let's say that on your vacation, you visit a public garden and happen to chat with a manager who's worked there for twenty-five years. You ask what books she has found particularly rewarding, and she enthusiastically names two that she adores and has read repeatedly. You write them down, together with her name and the date. *Voilà!* You're on your way.

Or let's say you meet a renowned professional in a particular field. Ask him for books he recommends. Once in a while you'll learn of a book that will transform you.

How to use book reviews

Most of the buzz about book reviews concerns whether they are favorable or not. But how relevant is this single opinion going to be to you?

It serves as one knowledgeable viewpoint to consider, but I recommend looking at reviews primarily as notices: *this* book of fiction or nonfiction is now available, it is written by *this* author and about *this* subject for *this* audience. Approached like this, reviews perform a valuable service. That the book is reviewed at all is a mark of distinction, since only about two percent of books published each year get reviewed.

If you are intrigued by the review, you may want to clip it, save it inside the book, and read it again after you've read the book yourself and formed your own opinions.

Rediscovering a national treasure

One of the best ways to learn what books are available is by visiting a public library. This seems like such an obvious statement, yet it is surprising how many busy booklovers I've met who have not been in their local libraries for years. Like our national parks, our public libraries constitute a treasure that many Americans take advantage of hardly at all.

Even if you prefer to buy rather than borrow books, libraries are enormously valuable for adding to your List of Candidates. While you'll find sections titled "New Fiction" and "New Biography," similar to what you'll see in your neighborhood bookstore, you'll also find books of merit that are no longer in the bookstores. Merely wandering through the stacks and observing categories is an adventure, as you take the measure of your interest in subjects you may have forgotten about. A library is a fueling station for your mind.

And while there is much to be gained simply by browsing in a library, there is even more to be gained by talking with the librarians.

The reader's service no one knows about

Most of us are familiar with the library reference desk and might go there with questions such as, "Where can I find information on penguins?" But some librarians can handle questions whose answers are more elusive—like this one: "Can you help me find more books like the one I read a while back? I don't remember the title or the author, but it took place in New York City around 1900, and the main character was a psychologist trying to solve a murder mystery."

Believe it or not, some skilled and patient librarians are specially trained to answer just such questions. They practice a little-known form of information science called Readers' Advisory, availing themselves of special reference works, in print and online, such as *What to Read Next, Novelist*, and that aptly named tribute to genre fiction, *Genreflecting*.

Using these and other indexes, the Readers' Advisory librarian can rather quickly confirm that the book was *The Alienist* by Caleb Carr. "Oh, and good news. Carr has a more recent book out, and here is a synopsis of it if you would care to read it. And since you like his work, you might also like these three authors...."

Readers' Advisory librarians are trained to interview patrons to determine what kinds of books they like—for instance, books with lots of character development or ones with fast-paced plots and plenty of action. They are trained to be nonjudgmental about reading tastes. Whereas some folks may look down on romance novels or westerns, Readers' Advisory librarians will help patrons find the authors within those genres that are likely to please them the most. It's comparable to handselling, the kind of personal service a good bookseller extends to customers, but even more intensive.

Imagine the new authors and topics you might learn about by spending a little time with such a specialist. Even if your librarians are not trained in Readers' Advisory, they can connect you with the reference guides, and you can do the exploring yourself. A delightful place to start is with *Book Lust: Recommended Reading for Every Mood, Moment, and Reason*, by über-librarian

Nancy Pearl. I've picked up dozens of new candidates from her impassioned recommendations.

Blessed be the guides

In my research, I perused a good number of guides to classic literature and was surprised at what I learned. I had a notion that the authors of these works might themselves be like dusty old books. Quite the opposite is generally true. Often they have a keen sense of irony and humor. They are passionate about the classics and in some happy cases, quite able to pass on their enthusiasm in an infectious way. Some of their guidebooks deserve to be part of your reference library—not as required reading, but as friends to be consulted for ideas and opinions.

One little gem that's been published in many inexpensive paperback editions through the years is *Good Reading: A Helpful Guide for Serious Readers*. It was created by a group of scholars, editors, and writers called the Committee on College Reading, which began in the mid-1930s and lasted for some thirty years. The chairman of this group was Atwood H. Townsend, a professor at New York University.

From his introductory essay, "On Reading," Professor Townsend comes across as a kind and wise fellow who's not shy about lecturing us. "No matter how busy you may think you are," he tells us, "you must find time for reading now, or surrender yourself to self-ignorance." Most comforting was this advice: "Never force yourself to read a book that you do not enjoy. There are so many good books in the world that it is foolish to waste time on one that does not give you pleasure and profit."

Good Reading is still available in the used-book market for practically nothing. What a treasure it can be to have Professor Townsend occupying a half-inch on your shelf, a trusted guide forever at your service for a suggestion or two on scores of classics.

In contrast to this group effort, consider another book called *The Lifetime Reading Plan* by Clifton Fadiman, published in 1960. Fadiman, who died in 1999 at the age of ninety-five, was one of the most widely read Americans. He was an editor of the *Encyclopædia Britannica*, a judge for the Book-of-the-Month Club, and a book review editor for *The New Yorker*.

Fadiman's pick of the one hundred best books, which include works by Pascal, Milton, and Eliot, are what Charles Van Doren defined as classics: books that do not have to be rewritten. Unlike most books, these have the capability of being "tools of self-discovery," as Fadiman described them. "That is, they bring into consciousness what you didn't know you knew." By reading these classics, Fadiman said, "we will have disenthralled ourselves from the merely contemporary."

As much as I admire his book, it's hard for me to imagine following Fadiman's plan from beginning to end. To abdicate your responsibility to create your own list would be a mistake, in my opinion. And besides, why deny yourself the same kind of fun that Fadiman had in creating his list? Nevertheless, I treasure his *Lifetime Reading Plan* on my reference shelf. When I do get around to reading *The Iliad* and *The Odyssey*, I'll come back to his sleek black volume and read his thoughts with great anticipation.

A more recent tour guide to our reading life is Harold Bloom, a professor of humanities at Yale. In *How to Read and Why*, Bloom describes "the second birth of the mind" that comes from a full reading life. Another scholar, this one a professor at Columbia, is Andrew Delbanco. In his *Required Reading: Why Our American Classics Matter Now*, Delbanco laments the dissection of literature that makes literary criticism irrelevant to those who read books merely for pleasure. He says, "I believe it is the responsibility of the critic to incite others to read them." He has certainly done so with me. His book is another that whispers behind my shoulder as a trusted and friendly guide. Delbanco unabashedly loves the classics and writes with clarity and charm. I look forward to his ready companionship on my future literary travels.

When to read a classic

Perhaps you've regretted, as I have, not having read more of the classics earlier in life. Yet plenty of the best literary tour guides assure us that reading the classics when you're older and more experienced can deliver richer benefits than reading them when you're young. The writer Anna Quindlen reminds us that "force-feeding" the classics to students often backfires, with students turning away not only from these books but from reading in general. "At age thirteen," she writes, "*David Copperfield* often seems less of an invitation to *Bleak House* than a clarion call for Cliffs Notes."

What's more, classics merit reading at various stages in your life—that's one of the hallmarks of a classic. Read *Romeo and Juliet* (or see the play) when you're fifteen, and every ten years thereafter, and it will mean different things to you each time. The author David Denby went so far as to return to college thirty years after his first tour to repeat the Great Books curriculum at Columbia University.

Created at Columbia early in the twentieth century, this curriculum, which covers the standard European literary and philosophical canon, spread first to the University of Chicago and then to many other American colleges by midcentury. He concluded that reading and re-reading the classics were both relevant to our present time and immensely rewarding. His *Great Books* is another valuable guide to your reading.

Reading with the ages

One of the wonderful things about the classics is that so many people have read them over the years. After you have read one, you can enter into a discussion free of the bounds of time. The great guidebooks to classic literature age slowly and gracefully. Even when quite old (such as *The Book-Lover*, published in 1885), they can be fascinating for discovering how the praise of a classic has changed—and how it has remained the same.

For me, the classics of literature are similar to the classics in music. Certain pieces I find astoundingly beautiful and others utterly boring. Follow your own tastes, mind, and heart, and use your pick of learned guides to help you enjoy more thoroughly the books that will become *your* classics.

Your new bicameral library

No matter how old or young you are, you can take pleasure in your growing two-part library. Your Library of Candidates provides the source of satisfying new books. Here is where acquaintances wait to become friends. Once you've read a book, it moves to your library of friends, or what I call your Living Library. I like the name Living Library because your books will continue to speak to you as you refer to them over the years.

John Armato, a public relations executive, cherishes his growing Library of Candidates. When people ask him if he's actually read all those books, he asks them if they've actually eaten all the food in their kitchen. "It is good to put up a supply of books; it increases the odds that you'll have what you want when you're hungry for it," he says.

How you organize your Library of Candidates is a matter of personal style. John mixes his candidates with those he's read to keep all the books on a subject together. As I mentioned, I prefer separate shelves for my Library of Candidates, which I group by category. Andrea Syverson, a marketing and branding strategist, keeps her large Library of Candidates in its own room. "It's like having my own mini-bookstore," she says.

Tim Sanders, business guru and most energetic reader, keeps his Library of Candidates at home and his Living Library at work. "The workplace library makes it easy for me to refer to books while doing business and allows me to be more productive with my downtime," he writes in his book, *Love Is the Killer App*.

Having your Library of Candidates easily accessible means that you can quickly take up the book that hits the right spot just when you want. If I'm choosing a book for a plane trip, I take one that I can read in the noisy, unpredictable environment of airports and airplanes. When I can read in more comfortable circumstances, I'll select the more intense books, which I'll want to read while taking notes.

It is said that youth is wasted on the young. Perhaps. And is age wasted on the old? One way to grow with your years is to grow with your List of Candidates, your Library of Candidates, and your Living Library. This way you will always be learning. All the fascinating and vigorous older people I've known have one trait in common: an intense curiosity that propels them to learn more and more.

Allocating time for your lifelong learning

Developing your List and Library of Candidates takes a little time. Is it worth it? Think of the time you spend reading. Whatever that is, would you spend five percent of that time in planning if by doing so your rewards could be magnified many times over?

When you allow your reading choices to be ad hoc and accidental, it's hit-or-miss in terms of how much you enjoy and learn from them, and how meaningful books become in your life. When, however, you plan most of your reading by actively seeking good books, by considering a wider range of titles, and by choosing more carefully, your rewards are going to go up. Most probably *way* up.

As your List and Library of Candidates grow, they will give you food for thought each time you turn to them. And as you begin to read these books, they will, perforce, lead to other books and other interests. Interests are like candles, each one capable of lighting more without diminishing itself.

Your candidates become the curriculum of your own lifelong learning that can lead you to a far richer life. As the saying goes, if you don't know where you're going, any direction will do. When you do begin to plan your reading life, not just any book will do. Life is too short, and *your* list of good books beckons.

Should all your reading be planned? Of course not. Plan to the extent that feels right to you at a particular time in your life, but always be open to serendipity. Take up those books that seem to find you. Put out-of-the-blue titles on your List of Candidates even though they seem to fit nowhere. These are zesty additions because they are exceptions to your planning—that's what makes them so sweet.

If you have floated about with the typical casual approach to finding your next book, imagine what a profound change you can make in your life by taking charge of your book selections. It's the difference between merely drifting and actually going places.

A life energized by books

Someone who sees all the books in my home might conclude that I prefer pages to people. Far from it. The point of reading is not reading but living. Reading helps you live with greater appreciation, keener insight and heightened emotional awareness. For proof, look to the innumerable great readers who have been great doers, from John Adams to Teddy Roosevelt to Paul Theroux to George Plimpton. Reading and action reinforce each other in an ever-escalating manner.

Your well-read life is a path for living more fully. Louis L'Amour summed it up in six words: "Read, read, read. Do, do, do."

To be able to turn at will, in a book of your own,
to those passages which count for you, is to have
your wealth at instant command.

—John Livingston Lowes

2

Seizing More from Your Reading

In the many books on how to improve your reading, one point stands out: if you want to read well, read actively. Ask questions of yourself and the author. Engage in a dialogue.

As early as 1928, the scholar and popular writer Ernest Dimnet wrote in *The Art of Thinking*, "Whatever we read from intense curiosity gives us the model of how we should always read." A year later, Walter Pitkin wrote in his *Art of Rapid Reading*: "You will get little or nothing from the printed page if you bring to it nothing but your eye." Pitkin, a professor of journalism at Columbia, advised readers to ask themselves, "Just why am I going to read now? Just what do I want to get out of it?"

Engaged, active reading

Probably the most famous proponent of active reading was the philosopher Mortimer Adler. His *How to Read a Book*, first published in 1940 and revised in 1972, became the twentieth century's classic text on the subject. "One reader is better than another in proportion as he is capable of a greater range of activity in reading and exerts more effort," Adler says. He is better if he "demands more of himself and of the text before him."

So what does a reader do, besides asking questions, to read actively and demandingly? The advice-givers all agree that you should *not* start by reading the first sentence of a book and then plow your way through to the end. Instead, begin by previewing the book.

Start at 35,000 feet and gradually come in closer. Take stock of the book as a whole. Is the author's background in academics, journalism, or something else? Is there an index? A bibliography? If so, what do they reveal about the book? (Most of the advice on how to read is aimed at nonfiction works, although many of the techniques can also apply to fiction.) Look at the table of contents. Is it merely suggestive or is it detailed enough to be an outline? Are there illustrations that can serve as windows into the book?

Take this kind of cursory inventory of the book, which should last only a few minutes. Then close the book and think for a moment about these ingredients and what they mean. At this point you might reflect on what you already know about the subject and what you expect to learn from this book.

After this first look, conduct your second tour through the book. Read a bit of the front and back matter. Who seems to be the intended audience? If there's an index, scan its major headings to see which topics get the most coverage. Has the book been reprinted or revised? If so, during what span of years? Again close the book and let things sink in for a few moments. (You might find it useful to ask questions out loud during this process.)

Then take a third tour, and read a few introductory and concluding paragraphs from each chapter. That is where most writers sum up their major points.

It's as if you were stripping the book back to the outline the writer may have followed. With such an approach, Adler says, you can gradually construct your own outline for the book and are thus able, in your own words, to construct the author's points. If you plunge in from the opening sentence, you risk putting too much energy in the wrong place. Often the real meat of a book is some-where in the center, while the author added opening chapters to put things in context.

You also put your motivation in jeopardy when you just plunge in from the first. What happens if you quickly come across some-thing that is unclear? You might go make a sandwich and never return. Better to let your brain work more naturally by getting a general idea of the entire book first. Then when you come across things you don't understand (there will likely be fewer of them), you'll have the all-important benefit of context. Or the author may have some great ideas, but may present them in an order that hinders rather than helps.

I also find it useful to read capsule biographies of authors before reading their books, to gain a basic understanding of their perspective. A literary encyclopedia and biographical dictionary can work wonders in this regard.

Why superficial reading works

Cognitive psychologists as well as our own experiences tell us that memory is helped by building anticipation. Previewing the book, hovering over it at stages, builds your expectation for what you will encounter in the actual reading. Your mind likes this approach. You're creating places to put the facts and concepts that are to come, like putting clothes in a well-organized closet.

Adler calls this "superficial reading," and deems it a good and useful thing. Take this high-altitude approach to pick up main ideas before engaging in "analytical reading," where you actually home in on the ideas.

It might seem that this successive approach would add time to your reading. In fact, it reduces the time it takes to absorb ideas and make them stick. In the end, you'll gain a more complete understanding of a book in less time.

When to give up on a book

So reading actively, with enthusiasm and passion, is key. If you cannot do this with a book, you probably should not read it at all. Many of us feel obliged to finish a book once we've started. It's a finish-your-plate mentality. Normally it's a positive attribute to follow through and finish the things you start, but it's generally wrong with a book that doesn't speak to you, no matter how highly others regard it. How many times have you suffered through a book, holding out some hope that surely it must get better, only to finish wondering, "Is that all there is? What in the world do others see in this?"

There is some merit in being sure that you dislike the whole of a book versus only the first part. But most avid readers I've interviewed have learned over the years the art of knowing when to give up. Many apply a fifty-page rule: if you don't like it after fifty pages, close the book and move on.

Scott Eyman, the book reviewer for the *Palm Beach Post*, receives an average of three hundred books a week. Somehow he winnows the pile down to two or three to read and review. His office is filled with stalagmites of books, stacked to their teetering points on every horizontal surface. On the day I visited, he managed to clear a chair so I could sit. My briefcase had to wait in the hall.

Scott explained that the obligation to sift through so many books forces him to be draconian in the selection process. He won't wait even for fifty pages. "If I hate it, or get bored, or if it just doesn't resonate with me, I'll heave it across the room," he said. "If I make it to page fifty, I'm committed."

A few years ago I gave up on *Crime and Punishment*. I found it not enough crime and too much punishment. I went beyond fifty pages. In fact, I went about two-thirds of the way through before I finally surrendered and accepted that one person's masterpiece may be another's misery. Now I give up on books at any point. I'm (mostly) over the clean-your-plate syndrome.

As encouragement for you to give up even on venerated classics if they don't speak to you, consider *Rotten Reviews* by Bill Henderson. Here you will find an entire volume of unfavorable reviews of works that are considered some of the best books of all time. Frequently, the bad reviews are written by literary lions. Here's Emerson on Jane Austen: "I am at a loss to understand why people hold Miss Austen's novels at so high a rate, which seem to me vulgar in tone, sterile in artistic invention, imprisoned in the wretched conventions of English society, without genius, wit, or knowledge of the world." No matter what treasured classic or highly praised new book you dislike, you almost certainly are not alone (and are often in venerable company).

To live your well-read life, you must choose lots of candidate books and sample them. Should you hesitate to give up on a book, remember the vast number of delightful books waiting for your attention—more than you will ever have time to enjoy. Why squander time reading books that don't speak to you?

How to retain more of what you read

I once asked a widely read friend of mine if she had read T. E. Lawrence's *Seven Pillars of Wisdom.* Yes, she had. When I asked her what she thought of it, she could remember only that it had something to do with Arabs.

What's the point of having read a book if you can't remember a thing from it?

If you want to leverage your reading comprehension, spend a little time with your books *after* you've read them. Savoring them, in a deliberate way, is the secret for getting far more out of your books and retaining the information for long periods. It's bringing out the colors and fixing them as in an oil painting, rather than letting them wash away like colored chalk on a sidewalk.

Just as most people do themselves a disservice by not putting more care into the selection of their books, they also cheat themselves by closing their books too soon, rather than cooling down with them and employing a few techniques that will let them blossom in their memories. Lewis Carroll, who was a distinguished professor of logic and mathematics at Oxford in addition to being the creator of *Alice in Wonderland*, once gave a talk on how to gain more from books. Allow time, he advised, for reading to percolate through your mind. "One hour of steady thinking over a subject (a solitary walk is as good an opportunity for the process as any other) is worth two or three of reading only," he said.

It depends on your purpose, of course. If you are reading to pass time, then it matters little what you remember. You may wish only to keep track of the title and author to avoid starting the same book again. If you are reading with the intention of learning, then it's a whole different story. That's where, with a little know-how, you can greatly enhance a book's long-term value to you.

The first step to retention is to briefly review your book almost immediately after finishing it. It's easier if you've marked passages and taken notes in the margins and on the endpapers. You can then go through your book, reminding yourself why you marked the particular passages and wrote the commentary you did. This may encourage you to add to your marginalia or write longer notes elsewhere.

In David McCullough's *Path Between the Seas: The Creation of the Panama Canal, 1870–1914*, I found so many aspects fascinating that I wrote down my impressions to help fix them in memory. Years later I can recall Ferdinand de Lesseps, the French leader of great vision and strength who built the Suez Canal yet foundered in Panama, partly because he was too inflexible to see that the new obstacles he faced in Central America would not yield to the same tactics he had used successfully in the desert. His weaknesses, combined with his charisma, led to the biggest public stock failure in French history. And it was fascinating to learn how medical problems had to be solved before the engineering ones, and what skepticism the scientists faced when trying to convince the authorities that mosquitoes, not miasmic vapors, were actually responsible for malaria and yellow fever.

By taking my own notes, then reviewing them soon after I'd finished the book and a few more times after that, I planted these stories deep in my memory. I wrote the preceding paragraph without referring to my notes, five years after reading the book. Believe me, I am no whiz at such things. I simply had the motivation to remember, and I used some simple techniques to do so.

Besides writing and reviewing notes, I talked about McCullough's book with Lori and a few of my friends who were patient enough to listen to me rave about it. Memory researchers tell us that using as many of our senses as possible will help us remember things. Writing and talking and flipping through the book you've recently finished are all good ways to cement ideas in memory. So is conjuring up images that formed in your mind as you read various sections of the book.

Most of the techniques devised for reading and remembering the content of books have been designed for college students, but lifetime learners can successfully adapt many of them.

Proven techniques for remembering

In the 1940s Francis Robinson, a professor at Ohio State University, came up with something of a breakthrough for learning college course material. It is an eminently practical method based on psychological research that he called SQ3R: Survey, Question, Read, Recite, and Review. The idea is to survey each section of a textbook, starting out high and coming in lower for successive passes. Key to this method is transforming the textbook's subheadings into questions. "Naturalistic Substage" becomes "What Is the Naturalistic Substage?" Then read to answer the questions, practice reciting the answers without looking at the text, and after short breaks, review what you've learned.

At about the same time that Robinson was developing his method, a scholar named Edmond Bordeaux Szekely, who had studied and lectured at the Sorbonne, came up with his own, similar method for extracting the most from texts. In *The Art of*

Study: The Sorbonne Method, Szekely recommends that you underline key passages on the page of the text, write pithy summaries of these points in the right margin, and then write your own questions that these points answer in the left margin. Use the top margin for your own ideas and the bottom margin for things you don't understand. By covering up all but your prompting questions on the left, you can practice your recitation. Later, your notes at the bottom about the points that were unclear may become your most valuable notes of all. "In this way you become your own examining professor and your own judge," says Szekely.

Current college-level recommendations carry on the same basic idea: to learn most efficiently, you need to become your own instructor. Walter Pauk is the creator of the Cornell System for taking notes. With this method, students leave a wide left-hand margin for the questions they ask *themselves* after class or after reading, which their notes answer. Students then cover up the answers until they can recite them. In the seventh edition of his *How to Study in College,* Pauk still recommends his question-in-the-margin method for twenty-first-century students.

Whatever you wish to remember after finishing a book, it will help if you frame questions that will elicit these facts and ideas. Returning to *Panama,* for example, I asked myself: "What was the startling, counterproductive practice hospitals were following for their malaria patients?" Answer: "Putting bedposts in pans of water to keep ants away—meanwhile breeding mosquitoes in hospital wards." This is a proven way to seize the most from your reading.

After learning something, how best can we retain that information for the long term? The college study books pay lots of attention to this question, and one overriding lesson is to recite *soon* after learning something and then repeatedly, at lengthening intervals, as often as you need. Usually it takes surprisingly little time to do this, and you can retain an impressive amount of information for years to come.

College texts still refer to the pioneering work in memory that Hermann Ebbinghaus did in the late nineteenth century. A German psychologist, Ebbinghaus discovered that most memory loss occurs very soon after learning something. The best way to counteract this natural loss is to refresh your memory quickly—for example, later in the same day. Then refresh by recitation the next day, then perhaps a few days later, a week after that, and again at three weeks. These reviews, which may take only minutes, will yield surprisingly good results for your long-term retention. While this technique applies mainly to textbook and nonfiction learning, there's no reason you can't use it to remember the characters in *To Kill a Mockingbird* if you wish.

"The time you spend in reading is an investment," Walter Pitkin advises us. "You ought to get good returns on it. But, in order to do so, you must salt down the essence of books and articles in whatever form proves most usable." And don't put your notes away. "A notebook is not a miser's sock in which treasure is to be hidden," he reminds us. "It is a tool drawer, which ought to be opened daily."

Après Reading

One way to make it easier to review the books you have read is to designate Après Reading areas for them in your bookshelves.

Consider having one section for the books you just finished, where they will await your first review. These books should remain closed no longer than a few days before you review them. Then assign another location for a second-round review that you might do in a week or so. Finally, set aside a last shelf to review your books six months or so later. After this third review, go ahead and shelve your books wherever you want in your Living Library.

Another way to help your long-term retention is by keeping a reader's journal or annotated Bookography. The more you annotate the list of books and the dates you read them, the more you'll possess them. With a quick review of books from years past, you can refresh your memory of the points that were important to you. In fact, you can develop a memory of your books that may astonish people—most important, yourself.

Connecting with others through books

A marvelous way to retain your knowledge of particular books, as well as doing a bit of good in the world, is to buy extra copies of your favorites to give away. Sometimes one particular section is what spurs you to give the book to someone. If so, inscribe the book to them and add a note about page such-and-such. I've done this with some of my favorites, such as *The Richest Man in Babylon* by George S. Clason, which I give to young people since it encourages them to save ten percent of their pay and be thrifty. I give the philosopher Tom Morris's *True Success* as the best prescription I've found on how to accomplish your goals and live the good life. Recently, I've sent friends copies of *The Tipping Point* by Malcolm Gladwell, just because it's so interesting.

Some of the most creative and inspired people I've met recommend and give away books with a passion, including Mike Vance, the former dean of Disney University and the coauthor of *Think Out of the Box*; Paul Saffo, a director of the Institute for the Future in Menlo Park, California; and the *Killer App* author Tim Sanders.

It always pays to increase your vocabulary

At the risk of stating the obvious, the better your vocabulary, the more you'll enjoy your reading and the more you'll take from it. Not being sure of a word will slow you down as you try to infer its meaning from context (and you may be wrong). Who hasn't been guilty of plowing ahead with a guess? I've done it thousands of times, but guessing isn't nearly as satisfying as knowing. Moreover, once you learn a word, you tend to see it again, sometimes surprisingly quickly, which is a sign of what you've been missing all along.

In recent years I have become enamored of my computerized unabridged dictionary. When I have my computer with me (which is most of the time), in just seconds I can look up a word. I also can hear the word pronounced and then bookmark it to make later review easy. Periodically, I go back to my bookmarked words to check my retention. When I can't easily look up a word, I will underline it and write "Vo" in the margin—my reader's mark for a vocabulary word to look up later.

Improving your vocabulary can be a joyful lifelong endeavor that can provide a frequent source of satisfaction as you learn not only conventional words but also idioms and slang. I find my computerized, speaking dictionary particularly satisfying for French words such as *sangfroid* and *roman à clef*, which I learned just recently.

Recitation for an audience of one

People used to quote aloud from memory far more than we do today. Before the phonograph and talking pictures, before radio and television, before today's ubiquitous recorded music, people were obliged to entertain themselves. Memorizing poems and sometimes astonishingly long sections of prose was common, and recitations at a gathering could bring people a kind of pleasure unknown to those born in later eras.

Recently I decided to memorize a few short poems. I had memorized verse only once before, in ninth grade. It felt good to do it again, like stretching after being cooped up for a long time. It was satisfying, more than I had imagined, to be able to recite these short poems aloud while I was alone in the car or walking. The process engenders an appreciation for good writing that's hard to get any other way. Frost wrote, "Whose woods these are I think I know," not, "Whose woods are these I think I know." Memorizing makes you focus on nuance. Choose something to memorize from your favorite books and rediscover that old-fashioned pleasure.

Re-reading

Some of the most satisfying reading of all is re-reading. The Bible is the most re-read book of all in the West. Many people re-read it all their lives, gaining more from it as they mature. Many other books have served this purpose. Charles Darwin took Milton as a companion on his *Beagle* voyage. H. L. Mencken read *Huckleberry Finn* annually for years. Max Perkins, the editor of Fitzgerald, Hemingway, and Wolfe, re-read *War and Peace*

45

throughout his career at Scribner's. The text stays the same; the reader changes. One of the hallmarks of great books is that they continue to reward, time after time.

The truth about speed reading

Back in the 1960s, speed reading was hot. I remember Evelyn Wood Reading Dynamics newspaper ads and even billboards. Speed reading was taught at Helix High School, in La Mesa, California, where I attended ninth grade. I remember Mr. Schwendiman projecting text up on a screen in our darkened class-room and my feeling of dismay as the blocks of words flashed by at ever-faster rates. There was nervous laughter and heads looking around to see if anyone could actually read that fast. I think my reading did speed up temporarily (probably from fear of Mr. Schwendiman). I doubt, however, whether it had any lasting effect.

In the Space Age '60s, speed reading was seen as a scientific way to train people to cope with the ever-increasing amount of information. Yet today, in our Information Age, you don't hear much about speed reading. You can still find Evelyn Wood training sessions, but they have withered from six-week courses to one-day seminars. What happened?

It turns out that speed just isn't that important. It is no magic cure for information overload. You *can* increase your speed, even dramatically, but pure speed is only part—and not the biggest part—of reading well.

By the time Mortimer Adler revised *How to Read a Book* in 1972, he had to respond to what he termed the "fad" of speed-reading courses. He agreed that they are useful in letting your reading speed be limited by your mind and not your eyes. By simply using your fingers together as a pointer and disciplining yourself to read in this fashion, he wrote, you can read twice or three times as fast. Speed reading, says Adler, can improve elementary comprehension—that is, what a book *says*. But speed reading can't help you understand what a book *means*. That, says Adler, is controlled by your thinking speed, not your reading speed. Go ahead and take a course, he allowed; it won't hurt you. But it won't help you all that much either.

Speed reading is no more likely to make you a good reader than the ability to run quickly will make you a good tennis player. None of the professional readers I've interviewed—editors, writers, publishers, booksellers, book reviewers—believed that a speed-reading course made any difference for them. In fact, a surprising number said they consider themselves slow readers (although this is obviously a self-assessment). Only two people I've interviewed, both attorneys, reported that they profited by a speed-reading course. They use their skills today mainly for reviewing lengthy legal documents.

When you think about it, aren't some of the most important moments in reading, whether for pleasure or for learning, when you stop and gaze off with that faraway look? At these moments, your reading speed slows to zero, but your understanding soars. Oliver Wendell Holmes said, "The best of a book is not the thought which it contains, but the thought which it suggests: just as the charm of music dwells not in the tones but in the echoes of our hearts."

Evelyn Wood herself, when asked if she could really read a novel at 15,000 words per minute, answered, "Of course. But who would want to?"

Developing a flexible eye

In defense of speed reading, many of its techniques can help slow readers become faster, and can help all readers more efficiently comprehend the gist of expository writing. These techniques include eliminating regressions (when your eyes flit back to catch words and phrases you didn't get the first time), eliminating sub-vocalization (when you form the words subliminally while reading), and expanding your fixation length (the span of words you can see in a single glance), so that you're reading phrases rather than words. In his 1995 *Study Is Hard Work*, William H. Armstrong tells us that "one year of serious practice, training your eyes to take in more at each fixation, will reward you for the rest of your life."

Norman Lewis, the author of the highly regarded text *How to Read Better and Faster*, stresses the importance of being flexible in your reading speed. He agrees with Mortimer Adler and Evelyn Wood that we should read different books at different speeds, and different speeds within the same book, depending on our goals.

So don't think you're missing something by not taking a speed reading course. But do try to improve your skills at reading different material at different rates. Develop an easy loping speed for simpler material, and be able to slow down when the going gets tougher. Expect to have more technique and more flexibility as you mature as a reader, much like a musician matures in technique and flexibility. Isaac D'Israeli, the father of the British prime minister, said that just as there is a method to thinking and writing, "there is an art of reading." You can improve at that art all your days.

Why you should write in books

When in the trance of good fiction—when one is carried away by a story—writing in a book is unnecessary and can even be distracting. It is in expository writing, when one is reading to learn, that writing in books is so very helpful.

If you already write in your books, I encourage you to do even more of it and to take this art to a higher level. If you do not write in your books, I urge you to start, even though I know it goes against the grain.

I wrote a column for the Levenger Web site on this subject, describing those who write in books as Footprint Leavers and those who do not as Preservationists. Within a week, more than two thousand readers responded with arguments, many of them quite eloquent, either for or against leaving footprints. Ironically, both camps based their reasoning on a fervent love of books.

"A book unmarked is a book unloved," pronounced one Footprint Leaver. "An unmarked book is like a canister of undeveloped film, an unopened bottle of wine, a violin with sagging strings," said another.

Preservationists felt otherwise. "I never would write in a book, my thoughts are just that, my thoughts. Books should be left in a pristine condition. Notes are for notebooks," said one Preservationist. "It just makes me cringe to think about writing in a book of mine or even turning down the page to mark your place. That's what bookmarks are for!" insisted another.

Other people were in the middle and sometimes conflicted, as this reluctant Preservationist was:

*Alas, I am a Preservationist. I have tried numerous times
to be a Footprint Leaver, but have failed miserably!
I would love to be able to write in books; I just can't bring
myself to do it.*

For such wistful readers, today's stick-on notes allow them to write in books without actually doing so.

Many Footprint Leavers claimed that writing in books enhanced their understanding and memory, echoing various thinkers on the subject. Back in 1930, John Livingston Lowes, a Harvard professor of literature, recommended that readers use the flyleaves, or front endpapers, of books to list by page the topics that interested them. (Endpapers are the blank pages at the very front and back of a book.) Wrote Lowes:

*One cannot begin too soon to buy one's own books, if for no
other reason (and there are many more) than the freedom
which they give you to use their fly-leaves for your own
private index of those matters in their pages which are
particularly yours, whether for interest, or information, or
what not—those things which the index-makers never by
any possibility include. To be able to turn at will, in a book
of your own, to those passages which count for you, is to
have your wealth at instant command, and your books
become a record of your intellectual adventures, and a
source of endless pleasure when you want, as you will,
to turn back to the things which have given delight, or
stirred imagination, or opened windows, in the past.*

Ten years later, Mortimer Adler concurred that we should use the endpapers for our personal index, and further suggested that we use the front endpapers to record the thoughts that the book inspired. Whereas a bookplate indicates financial ownership, said Adler, writing in a book indicates intellectual ownership. And don't limit yourself to endpapers; if you respect an author, write throughout his or her pages:

> *Why is marking a book indispensable to reading it? First, it keeps you awake—not merely conscious, but wide awake. Second, reading, if it is active, is thinking, and thinking tends to express itself in words, spoken or written…. Third, writing your reactions down helps you to remember the thoughts of the author…. Marking a book is literally an expression of your differences or your agreements with the author. It is the highest respect you can pay him.*

Adler would have approved of John Adams's manner of reading. In his biography of America's second president, David McCullough tells us that Adams wrote no fewer than 12,000 words inside the covers of Mary Wollstonecraft's *French Revolution* (mostly disagreeing with the author).

Tracing footprints back to the beginning

Preservationists often feel that writing in books is somehow an affront to our intellectual inheritance and the proper respect that should be shown to books as carriers of our civilization. But writing in books was an important way of creating our intellectual inheritance in the first place.

Our religions and laws have evolved by means of innumerable handwritten notes inside of books, some of which over the years became incorporated into new editions of those books.

In addition to this natural evolution through which marginalia turns to print, scholars have made significant discoveries by examining the libraries of important thinkers. From reading what seminal writers and scientists have written in their books, scholars have been able to piece together the history of ideas.*

In the field of astronomy, for example, it was long believed that Nicolaus Copernicus's sixteenth-century work *De revolutionibus* (in which he put forth the revolutionary idea that the earth revolved around the sun) merely gathered dust for years. Yet as Owen Gingerich details in his ironically titled *The Book Nobody Read*, it was exactly the opposite: the book was read often, and we know this from readers' annotations.

In the history of mathematics, it was Pierre de Fermat's beguiling "I have discovered a truly marvelous proof, which this margin is too narrow to contain" that tantalized mathematicians for more than three hundred and fifty years, until 1993, when Fermat's Last Theorem was finally solved.

What to pass on to your family

Preservationists sometimes say they deny themselves graffiti gratification in order to pass on something of value. This is a noble gesture, but often based on faulty assumptions. For example, when the intended beneficiaries are family members, they may cherish

---

* For examples of historical reader's marks, some of which you may want to adopt, visit www.yourwellreadlife.com/footnote.

the books all the more for their marginalia, as these two Footprint Leavers explained:

> *Yes, I leave my mark. Never used to be that way until I lost some very special people in my life. Now when I come across notations that my father had once written, or a comment my husband jotted down, those scribbles bring back the person who left their mark in my life.*

> *I am so thankful that my own mother and grandfather "contaminated" many of their cherished books with their handwritten thoughts and feelings. I know them in a different way—an intimate way—through that ink.*

When the intended beneficiaries of unmarked books are libraries, Preservationists may be chagrined to learn that the chance of a library keeping their books (unless they constitute a rare and special collection) may be much lower than they think.

I learned this first hand years ago when packing up to leave Boston. I called our local library to announce our beneficent decision to donate some books. My philanthropic feeling was quashed when the librarian brusquely informed me: "First of all, we don't take textbooks, *Reader's Digest* condensed books, or any books with a distinct odor." She went on for a while with other caveats, drop-off restrictions, boxing requirements, etc., etc., until I managed to extricate myself from the lecture with a meek thank-you.

Now that I serve on the board of our local library, I understand that the books libraries receive from well-meaning patrons can be more burden than blessing. Librarians take great care (and also some professional pride) in selecting and preparing books for the public. The typical public library will enter into its collection only a small percentage of the books that it receives as donations. Most will be sold at modest prices (which can raise important funds), given to charity, or heaved into the trash.

The invisible legacy of Preservationists

In defense of Preservationists, they do often perform a great service to future readers. Even discounting family members, who probably would prefer some writing in the margin, and libraries, which most likely won't keep the books anyway, there is that growing world of used and out-of-print books increasingly accessible to readers via the Internet. Because of the pen abstinence of Preservationists, many readers, myself included, have acquired a bounty of unmarked old books.

And our country's heritage is indebted to one Preservationist in particular. Thomas Jefferson seldom wrote in books, contrary to his contemporary John Adams. His books formed the nucleus of our Library of Congress.

Beyond marginalia: turning books into journals

Some readers will write in the front of their books not only their name, but the date and place they began reading. These and other seemingly inconsequential temporal details—such as "on board the trans-Canadian railway from Toronto to Vancouver with the children, in Coach No. 5"—aid in memory.

Such notes can make your books something akin to scrapbooks or journals. They can become time capsules for you and others.

Have you ever come across an old ticket stub or other ephemera that you used as a bookmark and had a flood of memories come back? You don't have to leave these happy events to chance; you can plant them. Such cultivation of context can yield a harvest of memories in future seasons of your life.

On a trip to Amherst, Massachusetts, Lori and I toured Emily Dickinson's home. I bought a nice hardcover volume of her poetry in the gift shop and inside it wrote the date that we bought it, then taped in the ticket stub from the tour. Walking in Dickinson's yard with Lori that lovely summer afternoon, I picked up a perfect oak leaf from the grass and put that inside, too. Now our book is not simply any copy of Emily Dickinson's poetry, but a special one with particulars, and even a leaf from the very yard that inspired her.

Writing to authors

Another way to make books come alive with personal meaning is to write to the author. I find that writing a brief letter forces me to distill a few of the things I've liked best.

In writing my letter, which is simply addressed in care of the publisher, I'm careful not to exceed one page. I also usually quote a line or two that I thought was particularly compelling (a technique I picked up from *Cosmopolitan*'s legendary editor, Helen Gurley Brown). I don't ask for or expect an answer, although I receive one more than half the time.

I was inspired to do this back in graduate school, when I received letters from two authors I admired—Lewis Mumford and Ray Bradbury. Later on, two of my letters resulted in friendships I would cherish. One was with Otto Bettmann, who established the

Bettmann Archive of photographs. The other was with Stanley Marcus, whom I wrote to after reading *Minding the Store*, his history of Neiman Marcus. He became a longtime mentor.

You may be surprised at where your letters to authors lead. Whatever the result, keep a copy of your correspondence inside the book. What a treasure you create this way.

Hardcover books with dust jackets make surprisingly good storage containers. In the back you can put reviews, obituaries, printouts of email discussions you've had about the book, ticket stubs from the movie based on the book. The book becomes a special edition indeed—a one-of-a-kind—at least to you and most likely to your family members, who will someday open it to find treasure.

This isn't the only reason to buy hardcovers rather than paperbacks. It took me a while to discover this obvious fact, but the print on most paperbacks is more tightly packed and margins nearly nonexistent (except for high-quality trade paperbacks). Hardcovers make reading and writing easier. Sure, they cost more, but what huge benefits they deliver for an active reading life. They will reward you while reading and ever after as you revisit these old friends over the years.

Maturing into a fully adult reader

One of the pleasures of growing older is ending your formal education and taking full charge of your learning. At this stage (which we all hope lasts far longer than formal education) you go beyond trying to figure out what an author is saying. It is now more important to ascertain how an author speaks to you.

The utopian businessman and author Elbert Hubbard summed up this adult attitude about reading this way: "I do not read a book: I hold a conversation with the author."

You're studying your own topics for your own reasons now. You consider and skim many books to find what's useful and intriguing. With some, you reach in for a single piece of fruit. With others, you shake the tree with gusto. You have to be in charge of your own education to fully appreciate Bacon's adage, "Some books are to be tasted, others to be swallowed, and some are to be chewed and digested."

"The great secret of reading consists in this," said Charles F. Richardson in James Baldwin's 1885 *Book-Lover*, "that it does not matter so much what we read, or how we read it, as what we think and how we think it."

The more you bring to a book, the more you can take from it. Norman Cousins wrote: "The way a book is read—which is to say, the qualities a reader brings to a book—can have as much to do with its worth as anything the author puts into it.... Anyone who can read can learn how to read deeply and thus live more fully."

For the writer Henry Miller, reading was an act of creation. Upon finishing a book he would almost always write letters to friends, sometimes to the author, and occasionally to the publisher. He would copy out phrases in large letters and place them above his door so that his friends would see them. "The man who spreads the good word augments not only the life of the book in question but the act of creation itself," he wrote. "He breathes spirit into other readers."

Reading—the lifelong sport

"Reading is to the mind what exercise is to the body," wrote Joseph Addison in the eighteenth century. I think it's even better than that. While we should exercise our entire lives, we do not generally improve at physical activities after age thirty or so but merely retard physical aging. Reading is almost the opposite. If you have led an active reading life, your reading power at age eighty will tower over your reading power at age thirty.

What's more, the rewards of reading can accelerate like compound interest. Consider what it's like to read many biographies of twentieth-century figures. As each life unfolds, you learn how the same historical events, such as World War II, played out in the lives of Charles Lindbergh, FDR, Richard Feynman, Clare Boothe Luce, Nevil Shute, Joe DiMaggio, and on and on. You make connections and gain a view of history that is larger than the sum of its parts.

One of the most rewarding aspects of reading is that we can get better at it all our lives. Knowing how to approach books, increasing our capacity to understand them, using various techniques for reading actively, and remembering—these are part of what it means to be a fully adult reader. As you gain in experience, as your Living Library takes more shelf space, as your vocabulary expands, books that were difficult become easy. Books that you once understood at one level, you can now understand at more levels. Reading becomes easier and ever more satisfying as you progress. This gradual flowering into a fuller reader is one of the best things about getting older—and one of the best ways to ensure that, for you at least, age will not be wasted on the old.

Longfellow expressed beautifully what many lifelong readers discover:

> *For age is opportunity, no less*
> *Than youth itself, though in another dress,*
> *And as the evening twilight fades away*
> *The sky is filled with stars, invisible by day.*

When he was in his seventies, Carl Sandburg said, "All my life I have been trying to learn to read, to see and hear, and to write." And the master intellectual Johann Wolfgang von Goethe wrote, "The dear good people don't know how long it takes to learn to read. I've been at it eighty years, and can't say yet that I've reached the goal."

I think it's an essential need of the human being to hear another human being tell them a story....it makes us feel there's somebody else here with us.

—George Guidall

3

Reading with Your Ears

In 1993 I was reborn as a reader. It happened when I listened to my first audiobook, an abridgment of Roger Horchow's *Elephants in Your Mailbox*, about the lessons he learned at his mail-order business. I listened while driving to my own mail-order business, trying to pick up some useful information. And I did. But more important was what I experienced about audiobooks.

Up until that time, I had been a faithful listener to National Public Radio and had heard some awesome pieces of reporting, but it's hit or miss with radio, as you know. Once I learned of the wide variety of unabridged audiobooks available, my reading life changed forever.

It was under the spell of Frederick Forsyth's prose and the sound of David Case's voice reading *The Day of the Jackal* that I first exhibited that telltale symptom of one hooked on audiobooks: when I arrived at my destination I didn't get out of my car. I sat, like so many audiobook converts have done, unable to tear myself away.

In the first ten years of my audio existence, I listened to more than a hundred unabridged books and became a changed person. Despite leading a hectic life building a business and raising children, I was able to live a reader's life, too. My commute was not long—only twenty minutes—so I soon strapped on a Walkman while washing dishes, exercising, and washing the family cars. I gravitated to history and biography, some of my favorites being

William Manchester's Churchill biographies and everything by David McCullough. Then there was Scott Berg's *Lindbergh*, Ross King's *Brunelleschi's Dome*, and on and on. (I always buy the hardcover as well so I can make notes in it, and see the book as well as listen to it.)

After decades of feeling wistful about all the books I was missing, suddenly I was reading more and living more.

Once converted, I became a proselytizer. My father was my first target. Initially reluctant to give up his radio, he quickly got just as hooked as I and then shot past me in his consumption. He's read just about everything available by and about Churchill, and recently completed the three-volume *History of the Twentieth Century* by Sir Martin Gilbert. Our mutual listening has brought us closer, as we meet weekly over breakfast and discuss the lessons of appeasement, the aspersions cast at immigrants, the tendency to defame people who are ahead of their times, and other frailties of human nature. It's made me a more interested person. How many things can I be interested in and learn something about? That's the quest I now find myself on, and I expect to be on this quest for the rest of my days. Audiobooks unlocked the reading life for me.

Born in traffic

How appropriate that audiobooks came to life in Los Angeles. It was there that a critical mass of bad traffic, technology, actors, and an entrepreneur came together and gave birth to a new art form.

It was 1973, and Duvall Hecht, then a forty-three-year-old financial executive, had a problem. He had agreed to coach the University of California crew team. This involved driving south from his office in Los Angeles to the Irvine campus, a ride that took him on the notoriously congested San Diego Freeway, Interstate 5.

Talk radio wasn't as pervasive then as it is today, and National Public Radio was just building its audience. "I was bored with the lack of serious and sustained intellectual challenge," Duvall said. He yearned for the mental stimulation that only books could provide. How grand it would be, he thought, if he had tapes of people reading whole books.

Recorded books had actually been around since 1931, when Congress initiated the Talking Books Program to serve blind and physically handicapped people. And Caedmon Records had been recording authors reading their own works since 1952, when Dylan Thomas read his *Child's Christmas in Wales* and *Five Poems*. Listeners in homes and schools played these recordings on record players. But Duvall wanted books read in their entirety on cassette tapes, so that he could play them in a portable player in his car.

Back then, cars didn't have built-in cassette players. But players had recently become lunchbox size so that you could carry them in your car and run them on batteries or plug them into the cigarette lighter. That's how Duvall began his listening in the early 1970s. (It would take a few more years before built-in cassette players became more or less standard equipment, and until the end of the 1970s before a revolution in audio portability blasted onto the scene—the Sony Walkman.)

It was just before 1975 that Duvall started the Books on Tape company and launched the industry of renting audiobooks. Shortly after this, another audiobook firm began, created by a similarly frustrated businessman, a traveling salesman from Maryland named Henry Trentman. His company, Recorded Books, operated along the same general lines. Their key customers, both companies soon learned, were avid readers who wanted to get more books into their lives while driving.

Narrators from backstage

Actors were a logical choice for narrating the books. They had trained voices, lots of talent, and usually not a lot of work.

In 1979, Henry Trentman posted a note backstage at the Arena Stage in Washington, D.C., soliciting actors to record books. He struck gold. From that first call came veteran actors such as Alexander Spencer, Mark Hammer, and Frank Muller, all of whom became superb narrators. Muller went on to narrate four hundred books for Recorded Books and become one of the most popular voices of the new art form.

Most of the best narrators were stage actors, and they made stories come to life in ways that often surprised the publishers and even the authors. Listeners fell in love not only with the authors but with the narrators, whom they came to associate with the voice of the protagonist. This was especially the case with serial novels such as the Nero Wolfe mysteries of Rex Stout and the Travis McGee adventures of John D. MacDonald. The veteran actor Michael Prichard recorded both. (Interestingly, most of the fan letters that Books on Tape and Recorded Books receive are addressed not to authors but to narrators.)

Sometimes the fans are authors themselves. The bestselling author Jerry Jenkins told me how Frank Muller bowled him over. "I became so enamored that I began listening to everything he read, even if I wouldn't normally be interested in the subject," he said. When Jerry finally talked with Frank by phone, "I was just a groupie, gushing that I listened to everything he recorded." Jerry asked him to consider recording his *Left Behind* books, which Frank later did.

From zero to 60,000

In 1986 a trade association called the Audio Publishers Association began. Ten years later, the group established the Audie Awards for the best recordings of the year. From virtually nothing in 1975, audiobooks exploded to 60,000 titles by the end of the century. And by that time nearly a quarter of all American households had listened to an audiobook within the last year. A new art form—quite different from printed books, and also different from oral storytelling and radio theater—had arrived.

Do you fit the profile?

Who are those avid readers most apt to become avid listeners? "A person who is active eighteen hours a day, twenty-four seven, an A-type personality, a high-energy man or woman," says Duvall Hecht. Usually this person is over thirty or forty, he adds, because younger people are focused on building their careers and reading lots of trade and professional publications. "But at a certain point, when they are established, they realize there's a whole other side of life that needs development, and that's their intellectual life."

Says Robin Whitten, the founder and editor of *AudioFile* magazine: "It's busy people spending more and more time in cars."

An example of such an avid reader is Sarah Thomas, the director of the Cornell University Libraries. With an undergraduate degree from Smith and a Ph.D. from Johns Hopkins, Sarah has read her share of books and, not surprisingly, loves to read. She oversees the nineteen libraries at Cornell, with a staff of five hundred. Reading more books, she says, not only enriches her own life but allows her to relate to more of her patrons and staff. But like every busy professional and mother, she has only so much time to sit and read.

One of the first audiobooks Sarah listened to in the car was Peter Mayle's *Year in Provence*. She delighted in all the well-executed French accents. "I was surprised. I don't think that I had fully grasped the possibilities of the media. If you take something like *Three Junes* by Julia Glass, the story of a Scottish family, how much more alive the story comes with the Scottish accent than when you're reading the book and trying to imagine it."

Another serious reader whose life has been transformed by audiobooks is Jerry Galison. He founded the Galison company, which makes high-quality greeting cards for the museum market. Jerry lives in New York City and walks to work with earphones on. It's about thirty minutes each way, and he usually listens to biographies. "Many have knocked my socks off," he says. "For a few, particularly if it wasn't in the middle of a crowded street, I've stopped and applauded. With basically all, when the protagonist dies, I get teary. I consider it a wonderful part of my life."

Time lost—and found

There are many others like Sarah and Jerry—avid readers who have managed to fill their lives even fuller with the help of audiobooks. While commute times stretch out across America, an increasing number of people are listening to books and loving it. Those who study traffic congestion refer to these lengthening commutes as lost time. Robin Whitten has a different view. "From an audiobook perspective it's not lost time, it's found time," she says.

Duvall Hecht calculates that his top subscribers complete about a book a week, but that's rare. A good customer rents a book a month. How would your life be enlarged by twelve more books a year?

Other born-again readers

It's not only high-powered commuters who become audiobook lovers. Librarians testify to long-haul truckers checking out audiobooks by the boxload between trips that typically last for weeks. Audio publishers have received thousands of fan letters from telephone lineworkers, fence menders, letter carriers, tenders of crops and livestock, and others in manual occupations.

Artists and craftspeople, whose work involves short flashes of intense concentration followed by long hours of less mentally demanding work, often fill these hours with audiobooks.

These studio workers are actually following a long tradition of people who have paid money to have stories read to them. In the mid-nineteenth century, Cuban cigar makers hired a *lector de tabaquería* to read to them while they worked. One of the most popular books was Alexandre Dumas's *Count of Monte Cristo*. Visions of Mediterranean islands, lost love, and clashing swords so entranced the cigar workers that they ordered the book read again and again.

In 1870, the workers wrote to the author and asked his permission to name their cigars in the book's honor, which Dumas granted that year of his death. Thus was born the Montecristo cigar.

Then there are those who get so hooked that they look forward to necessary but mindless tasks around the house. I like washing dishes when I can listen to my book. I readily turn off my book when family members want to talk, but they also know my habit and usually leave me alone to clean up the kitchen in the evening. I also have washed our cars a lot more than I would have otherwise. I grew tired of moving cassettes from my car to my Walkman, so now I listen to one book in the car and another in my Walkman (or now, my iPod). Just as one can read more than one book at a time, I listen to more than one at a time.

Some listeners who had never made time for books in their lives have surprised themselves by becoming born-again readers through audiobooks. My father had been an avid reader only once for a short time, by accident, while in the U.S. Navy. As an eighteen-year-old quartermaster in 1945, he was shipped off to the Philippines just as World War II was ending. The Navy somehow lost track of him and as a result, he was able to spend weeks in a hammock reading all day long. Luckily, there was a small library on base. He blissfully blew through plays and novels, classics and contemporary works until the Navy caught its error and he was reassigned to a ship. There followed a forty-seven-year lull in his reading until he got hooked on audiobooks. Ten years after listening his way through some hundred and fifty books, at age seventy-six, he said:

I have more of a passion for learning now and more patience now—the opposite of what I was like sixty years ago. I'm probably a better student, with less capability now as a student, but a better one as far as attitude is concerned. I want to understand what the author is saying, I want to be able to swallow it so that I can measure it against my own intellect and see whether or not I agree with it, whether there are any flaws with it, whether or not I really learned something—all those things, which students should do. In my memory of fifty or sixty years ago I was just interested in getting by so I could get out of school and on with my life. The motivating factor as a teenager was money, not knowledge. Now it's just the reverse.

Four surprises about spoken books

In the first years of recording books for the general listener, there were some surprises. The first was that listening to a book while you drove did not merely occupy your mind but could calm it.

Once I began listening to books, I noticed that I lost my usual hot reactions to the craziness that goes on every day on the roads. This feeling is typical. "You just don't experience road rage," confirmed Eileen Hutton, the president of Audio Publishers Association. "When some idiot cuts you off, it just doesn't seem to matter as much when you're lost in a good book."

A second surprise was that authors are not usually the best readers of their own works. Writing and narrating are different arts. The likelihood of finding an author who can narrate is about the same as finding a dancer who can sing. It happens, but it's rare. George Guidall has recorded more than a thousand books. "My job is to really transform one art form into another. The written art form is the author's province. Spoken art form is mine." It's a type of acting, he says, but "you can't act an audiobook in the same way you portray a character. What I really am is the voice of the author." Like studio musicians, professional narrators command top dollar by being able to come in, sit down, and record without rehearsal, thus saving expensive studio time. The good ones are very good indeed and are hired to record hundreds of books.

One of the happy compromises being done today is to have the author record a brief introduction to the work, or even better, an interview at the end of the work. This way the listener does hear the author's own voice and may get further insight into the work.

A third surprise was music. While it's a critical ingredient in movies, theater, and radio, music is a distraction in audiobooks. Sometimes short musical passages—a few bars only—can be used effectively before a book begins or to set off chapters, but as background to the voice, it is a distraction.

A fourth surprise concerns the number of actors performing a book. Even when a book has many characters and lots of dialogue, it is usually better to have only one narrator. When audiobook producers try to enlarge the performance by using a number of actors cast in the various roles, the work starts to resemble a radio theater production. One is then tempted to add music and sound effects and recreate that art form. But books aren't radio scripts. Good narrators do change their voices slightly to indicate different characters, but the single voice retains the feeling of a book.

The voiced vs. non-voiced debate

A long-running debate in the audiobook industry has been whether it's better to give a fairly unanimated, so-called straight read, or whether narrators should put a lot of vocal variety into their reading, to emphasize the distinction between characters. This question is known as the voiced versus non-voiced debate. Wanda McCaddon, a stage actress who has narrated more than six hundred books, puts herself squarely in the voiced camp. "When I read, I hear voices and hear the people talking. How could I possibly read it without giving them voices?"

The answer lies in degree and balance. Claudia Howard, the studio director for Recorded Books, says narrators have to steer between performances that are too small or too large. She cautions aspiring narrators that in an audiobook, a little characterization goes a long way. "Often a suggestion of character is all that it takes," she says.

The first books were spoken

When the industry began, audiobooks were intended to provide a substitute for reading. It's come as a surprise just how good the substitutes are—in some cases, perhaps more satisfying than the printed books. While audiobooks may seem to be interlopers within the ancient domain of books, in fact it is the other way around. *The Iliad* and *The Odyssey* were passed down as oral history long before being committed to writing, as were *Beowulf* and many other stories. And when books were first created, they were designed to be read out loud, usually by representatives of the church, reading slowly to illiterate congregations. Written words were like written music, meant to be performed for the ears.

Early books of liturgy commonly intermixed music and words, indicating where in the service speaking and singing alternated.

When priests first began to experiment with reading silently to themselves, it was viewed as odd, if not suspicious, and even un-Godly. Yet we have lived with books and silent reading for so long that we are in danger of mistaking them for the native inhabitants of storyland. Audiobooks restore voice to the language that print mutely preserves.

When audiobooks are better than printed ones

Consider what happens to a book that features lots of dialogue, with many characters speaking in different dialects or with various accents. In the print realm, authors often read their manuscript aloud to make sure it *sounds* right. The reader then tries to reconstruct the voices, silently imagining how they sound. Sometimes, despite proper punctuation, one loses track of who is speaking, let alone how it might sound.

Contrast that experience with what happens in the audio realm. A small team of researchers first checks pronunciations, sometimes calling on experts for just the right way to say a town in India or a type of Chinese weapon or an article of sixteenth-century peasant clothing. The studio director then casts the narrator who can do the main accent with authority, while modulating his or her voice for the different characters. Instead of seeing quotation marks and indented paragraphs, we *hear* a narrator pause slightly and change voice slightly for the different characters.*

---

* For a multimedia account of my visit to Recorded Books' studios and how an audiobook is actually made, visit www.yourwellreadlife.com/footnote.

In some cases the author's ideas can reach us more directly and powerfully through audiobooks than through the intermediary of print. *AudioFile*'s Robin Whitten says, "There are occasions where the dialogue and dialect simply don't get across to the reader as well in print as they can in audio." She cites William Faulkner, whose long sentences and syntax, when spoken by the narrator Mark Hammer, "make the music that Faulkner intended." And in Zora Neale Hurston's *Their Eyes Were Watching God*, "again the dialect is hard, but in the voice of Ruby Dee or Lynne Thigpen, it's magical."

Sometimes an audiobook is what rescues a book from the unread pile. For Robin, that happened with the award-winning first novel of the Indian author Arundhati Roy, *The God of Small Things*. "I found I had a terrifically hard time with a lot of the names, and it slowed me down. I put the book aside even though it had won all those awards." But then she listened to the audio. "It became one of my favorite audiobooks and favorite books."

Heightened understanding can sometimes come from listening to a book *while* reading the text, especially if the language is archaic. Daniel Murtaugh, a professor of English at Florida Atlantic University and a Chaucer scholar, says it is worth the effort to read Chaucer in his Middle English, and so much easier if you listen to a good recording while reading.

Recorded Books' Claudia Howard says that every book has a voice; if it is cast well, the result can be a more complete experience of a book than merely reading the text.

> *In the hands of the proper actor, you will get nuances of*
> *cultural identity and vocal characteristics and dialect that*

you wouldn't get if you read it to yourself. You also get the added benefit of all the pronunciations done correctly, so that you are getting the reality of how these words are said and these names and these places. You don't look all that stuff up yourself when you read a book.

In my own listening, I have experienced a book-narrator combination so powerful that the narrator's voice is forever inscribed in my mind. The book was *Lolita* and the narrator, David Case. In his suave, effete English accent, David Case *was* Humbert Humbert, all the more so since the book is written in the first person. If I pick up the book and read a sentence, I hear Case. When I hear him narrate other works (which is easy to do, since he's recorded more than eight hundred books), I always see Humbert, and I have to wait until the new words and plot overtake my memory and I can enjoy him again as a fine narrator, rather than that adult lover of young Lolita.

The limitations of audiobooks

"We are a listening animal," Duvall Hecht reminds us. "The human animal has had millennia of listening to stories before there were books." As children, most of us delighted in hearing books before we ever read them ourselves. Yet Duvall concedes that some people are better aural learners than others, and that the affinity for audiobooks probably falls along a continuum. "There are some people who try it and just can't get into it—they like to read." Grover Gardner, a veteran narrator, agrees. "I know people who don't like it. They prefer to read for themselves, and they don't like someone else to interpret for them."

It is certainly true that listening to audiobooks takes longer than reading, since most people read faster than the speed of normal speech. Early in my listening career, I decided to tackle *War and Peace*. It came in four boxes, contained forty-five tapes and took me months to get through. Looking back, I wish I had used the printed book as a guide, as I do now. It would have helped to see the cast of characters laid out, and to *see* the Russian names as well as hear them, which would have made more of the novel stick.

Are you ristening?

When Gutenberg first set movable type, his detractors dismissed his innovation as a poor substitute for proper books hand-copied by scribes. We are still in the incunabula period of our aural history. Audiobooks are still viewed suspiciously by many readers today as not quite real reading.

One reason lies with our vocabulary. When we say we have "read" a book we mean that we've sat by ourselves and silently read the text of a printed book. We have no verb for listening to an audiobook, except "listening," and listening is something children do before they can read. Our editor at Levenger Press, Mim Harrison, another convert to audiobooks, has felt the inadequacy of our vocabulary. She and I now speak laughingly of "ristening" to books. The word sounds a bit odd, but so did "Ms." when we first heard that a generation ago. And doesn't a new art form merit a new word? I predict that the prejudice against audiobooks will pass as more readers experience the magic of being read to by gifted narrators.

A gift for our time

"I think it's an essential need of the human being to hear another human being tell them a story. I think it makes us feel that there's somebody else here with us," says the narrator George Guidall.

Once the optical ability to read passes, the lucky ones have had others read to them. Milton, blind at forty, had his daughters. That great reader of the twentieth century, Clifton Fadiman, in the end had his daughter, Anne, to read to him.

Now all of us can hear the books of our choice, read by superb artists, whenever we wish it, at any hour of the day. And we can enrich our lives with stories that we otherwise would never have known.

Reading confirms your aliveness. It's very validating. That's what book groups ultimately are; you get validated in the human condition—the conditions and puzzles, the good stuff and bad stuff, the aspirations and hopes and despairs. You're not alone out there.

—Rachel Jacobsohn

4

Sharing the Fellowship of Books

A neighbor of ours in Delray Beach is a voracious reader in her forties. She is married, has three children, and owns a decorating business. A few years ago she began a book group. "I had a couple of friends who had been in book groups before—one on Cape Cod and one in Tallahassee—and I bought a little book on book clubs and skimmed through it. It was more formal than I wanted, but I got a few good ideas and lists of books. I emailed my friends and got ideas from them and recruited ten or twelve girls, so you can usually count on eight being there, and it's a good thing."

In many ways our neighbor, Susan Hurlburt, is characteristic of the book-loving women who start groups. Typically, they have always loved to read and enjoy talking about books with family and friends. At some point they decide they want more of that kind of fellowship and start a group. Many thousands of people have started or joined such groups around the country in recent years. Yet this is not so much a new phenomenon as it is a continuation of a long tradition.

Mickey Pearlman, the author of the reading group guide *What to Read*, explains that reading groups started in colonial America in the form of women's study groups. In *The Reading Group Book*, David Laskin and Holly Hughes describe the women's "reading parties" prevalent in the early 1800s. After the Civil War, these women's groups spread throughout the country. Many of them evolved into various women's service organizations, but the germ of book discussion groups had been firmly planted.

Reading groups also resemble the kind of lifetime learning practiced in the American Lyceum movement, begun by Josiah Holbrook in the 1830s and carried forward by the Chautauqua movement later in the century. William Zinsser, in his book *American Places*, engagingly describes the lectures, readings, concerts, and discussions that began in Chautauqua, New York, and moved across the nation until the 1920s, when radio drowned them out. Today's reading groups carry on this American heritage in free self-education.

Viewed another way, reading groups provide more of what millions of readers get informally from friends and relatives: the fellowship of books.

Perhaps the most common kind of book conversations start with "Have you read such-and-such yet? It's really good!" Book groups expand on these spontaneous talks and ensure that the sharing and discussion become a regular part of members' lives rather than merely sporadic.

Yet, personally, the idea of joining a book group has long given me pause. I cherish selecting my own books. Why would I willingly join a group and lose some of that precious control? On the other hand, I love discussing books and know the power of those discussions for learning and retention. Book groups seem like the surest way to enjoy those benefits.

I was conflicted on this subject, so I decided to learn more about what the experience is like. I read a handful of guidebooks on the subject and then interviewed reading group members and leaders.

What the book group experience is like

Most groups, according to Rachel Jacobsohn, the author of *The Reading Group Handbook*, meet monthly for a couple of hours. They tend to take the summer off. Groups usually work best when there are between twelve and fifteen members, resulting in six to ten who actually show up for meetings.

Rollene Saal, the author of *The New York Public Library Guide to Reading Groups*, confirms that small is good, explaining that intimacy is best for discussion. She writes: "You want just enough people to sit comfortably in a roomy circle or around a big table."

Susan Hurlburt's group, which rotates its meetings among the homes of members, follows a typical pattern. "At first, I was a dictator," Susan confesses. "I got to pick all the books I was wanting to read—nonfiction, fiction, biography." Now, she says, everyone recommends a title.

Since her group doesn't meet in August, members try to pick a long book for September, such as *The Eustace Diamonds* by Anthony Trollope, at 800 pages, or Nancy Milford's *Savage Beauty: The Life of Edna St. Vincent Millay*, at 500 pages. They pick shorter books for November and December, when people are busy with the holidays.

Some groups specialize. There are groups that read just contemporary fiction or mysteries, spiritual books or business books, books by African-American or women authors. Other groups take pride in their wide-ranging selections. It's not unusual for groups to begin with a particular focus and then broaden their view over time. Fiction dominates in most groups because it is more open to interpretation, which tends to promote discussion.

Jerry Galison attends a book group that meets monthly over lunch at the Harvard Club in New York City. The group started with American colonial histories, but a couple of long, dry tomes caused Jerry to protest. He was promptly rewarded with the responsibility for choosing the books, which are now more varied. "I like to have at least one member, if not two, vouch for a book before selecting it," he says.

Book group members tend to have lots of education and life experience. Jerry studied at Harvard's Russian Research Center and has a fine-arts background in addition to business. The other members of his group, which includes men and women, have all been avid readers for many years. One woman, a retired book editor, "seems to have read everything," Jerry marvels, and really adds depth to discussions.

The members of Susan's group are all well-educated women, mostly in their mid- to late forties. One is an attorney and another a publisher. They don't have conventional nine-to-five jobs for the most part, and they all have children.

Karen Nakahara is part of a reading group in Philadelphia. She studied economics and French at Rice University and went on to get a master's in accounting. She was rising in the ranks at a major accounting firm before leaving to focus on her three children. All the members of her group are similarly well-educated moms. And, she says, "they like to read, not chat."

"We won't take the most popular book out there but something else—sometimes classics, sometimes new books," Karen says. They don't pick the most popular titles because members most likely will read those books anyway. That's a recurring theme among reading groups: most members read widely outside their book group selections.

No one knows just how many book groups are active in the United States today. Rachel Jacobsohn told me that she thinks the number is rising and estimates that there may be 750,000 or more, but she admits it's just a guess.

In a way, it's nice that there is no official count, for it reflects the purely volunteer, private, and refreshingly unofficial nature of reading groups. They report to no one and have no bureaucratic requirements. All this lends a certain tang of freedom to the experience. Book groups are exemplars of free speech and free assembly.

Many groups cherish this informality. Members are typically busy, and as Rollene Saal writes, "Once they have set aside the time for reading, they don't want to devote much energy to the administrative aspects of running a group."

Treasures you wouldn't have found

Before I began interviewing book group members, I figured I would hear complaints about their being expected to read books they didn't like. To my surprise, the benefit that members most often mentioned first was reading books they wouldn't have otherwise read—*and they liked almost all of them.*

Loie Williams, who has been part of a group in the Boston area for six years, told me simply, "I really enjoy it. I read books I wouldn't normally read." Jerry Galison reported that "we've read fifty books over the years, and I would say maybe four or five I would have read on my own." And most of them he enjoyed.

Getting more from books

The second benefit that reading group members mention almost universally is that they gain more from the book after discussing it with the group than they would have by reading the book on their own.

When she reads on her own, Loie Williams explains, "I don't often take the time afterward to chew it over and think about it. I have my next book ready, and I pick it up without really thinking about the prior book." But with her book group books, "even if I'm not enthralled with the book, I get different perspectives and think about it, and enjoy it, and get more out of it."

"A member will bring up a small little section and I might have missed the importance of it," says Susan Hurlburt. "Or you'll hear a viewpoint and think, 'I never thought about it, but you're right.'"

Jerry Galison shares a similar insight. "Sometimes after I had struggled with a book, I'd be embarrassed by the smart people who had read it and gotten so much from it."

Mainly women...but why?

While some groups, like Jerry's, have both women and men, the guidebooks—as well as the members I interviewed—indicate that most are women's groups.

I asked Susan Hurlburt if she would consider including men in her group. "No, not really," she said. "When I was starting it up, it was girlfriends. I can't think of many guys who read fiction. Guys don't talk about it as much."

Karen Nakahara explained that when her group got started, "no one really wanted men." When I asked why, there was a long pause. "Maybe…I really don't know why. Maybe because it would sway the discussion, or choices, and we'd think we should pick a book that the guys would like, too."

Maureen Boyle is a retired teacher who leads several reading groups around Delray Beach. "Men do read fiction, of course," she said, "but for some reason don't like to discuss it.

"Most men are interested in nonfiction," she continued, "and that's a little bit harder to have a book discussion around. I do have some men who come, but I've noticed that they have an inclination to be more silent; I think they are a little bit intimidated. Or occasionally a man will have a tendency to dominate, and you can see people withdrawing. They say, 'Okay, if he wants to dominate, I'll just sit back.' And that can occasionally happen with women, too. It's up to the leader to dampen it."

I asked several other women about the absence of men. One, after a typically long pause, lowered her voice conspiratorially. "You know, women have to deal with men in the other aspects of their lives, and we kind of like not having to in our reading groups."

Young mothers and great-grandmothers

Through my interviews and reading, I learned that young mothers figure prominently in book group membership. After stepping out of active careers to raise young children, many of them yearn for intellectual stimulation. Some of them turn to book groups as an oasis for their minds.

Another group that seems to take good advantage of book groups is older women.

Alice Robinson, who admits to being a near-octogenarian, is

a member of two groups that meet monthly in the Boston area.
A retired professor of history from Wellesley College, Alice comes
from a family of book group members. Her parents and in-laws all
belonged to book groups in Boston. One of those groups lasted for
one hundred and twenty-eight years.

When Alice was teaching, she was also raising four children,
mostly as a single mom, and soon after that caring for elderly
parents for twenty years. She didn't have time to read beyond her
professional responsibilities. Now she relishes her two groups and
misses them when she doesn't attend. "I definitely get more from
the books—from the different points of view.

"There was one recently, I don't remember the title, but there
was so much graphic sex in it that some of us got bored. I don't
think any of us are prudes but it was way overdone, although
some others didn't have that reaction." With Ann Patchett's
Bel Canto, the very different reactions of some of the members
prompted Alice to re-read the book to try to understand their
different viewpoints.

"I come away with a richer view of most of the books," she
said. "It's a good thing for me—keeps the brain cells going. I
intend to belong as long as I'm able."

Health clubs for the mind

For some of the members I interviewed, their book groups got
them to transform good intentions into real accomplishments. Like
joining a health club or exercise class, some people find it helpful
to take on the discipline of a group.

"Having a deadline and having to make a contribution to the

discussion got me back into reading," explained Dee Moustakas, who belongs to a group in Fort Lauderdale, Florida, that meets monthly.

A commercial writer and editor, Dee had always been a reader, counting it among her favorite activities. But she had fallen off in her reading when she was building her career.

Now in her early fifties, she told me it was during her thirties that her reading slowed to only a few books a year. "That's when I was really going gung-ho on my career," she said. "I read a lot, but magazines and trade books. It's funny—my house was full of books. I bought them; I just didn't read them. Thirty or forty percent had bookmarks halfway through. Now I finish them."

Being in her group has been "truly a life-changing experience," Dee said. "I'm proud that I've carved out the time to do it. It's so easy to say 'I don't have the time.'"

How *did* she carve out that time?

"This is silly…" Dee explained that she counts the pages she has to read for that month and divides by the number of days so she'll know her daily reading requirement. "When I come into the office in the morning, or first thing after lunch, I'll read the pages for that day. I read an hour a day, at least; I might read for several hours on the weekend."

What *isn't* she doing now? "I watch less TV, and before, I could always find something mindless to do in my office—a couple of games of solitaire on the computer, for example. I don't do that now. I don't think I ever wasted time, but I'm more efficient with my time now." She added, "I'm pleased that I've gotten back into something that was very meaningful to me."

Social side effects

Besides noting the concrete benefits—getting back into reading, reading books they would not have read, getting more from those books—members often comment that "it's more than just a book group." The social aspect of the group, which was *not* usually what got them to join, turns out to be important. They come to care for their fellow members.

"There exists a feeling of service and commitment to the group," says *The Reading Group Handbook*'s Rachel Jacobsohn.

Meeting time can be a reprieve. "Life outside of book groups is confusing, chaotic. Rules inside are clear and simple," Rachel explained to me. Members bond with former strangers and discover "a place where the intellect can be exercised with respect. I don't know how it *can't* change you."

Dee Moustakas relayed how, at one meeting, members described their successes and what they were grateful for. "You heard about grandchildren, or businesses, or volunteer work," she said. "Women don't always appreciate other women and it's a reminder that we're all successful in our own right. These women have become very important to me."

Public reading groups

Most reading groups form spontaneously and run independently and privately. But plenty of public groups also exist, usually based at libraries or bookstores. These public groups have several advantages over the private ones, including a wider range of members.

Diversity among members can be a good thing, Rollene Saal writes in her *New York Public Library Guide to Reading Groups*.

When you have members of different ages, genders, races—and not all friends, who tend to be more homogeneous—it can add "that little frisson of excitement and new interest."

My small public library in Delray Beach hosts several different reading groups, including Current Fiction, Mystery Lovers, and Understanding China (this last group changes its focus every year). According to the head of community outreach, Bonnie Stelzer, people like the diversity in membership. "People say to me that they have reading groups in their condos, but when they come to the library they get readers with different points of view. The library is a safe place where you can do that."

Reading the classics in the Great Books program

For those who want to read the classics, there is a small but venerable institution called the Great Books Foundation. It was started in 1947 by the president of the University of Chicago, Robert Maynard Hutchins, and his colleague Mortimer Adler, philosopher and author of *How to Read a Book*. The two of them had been guiding students through some of the classics and decided it would be good to design a program for adults outside the university who wanted to expand their minds.

In those early postwar years, plenty of returning vets and housewives wanted more of most things, including a life of the mind. The Great Books program, with its focus on the "Great Conversation," hit a responsive chord with the G.I. Bill generation. Groups formed across the country and continued to grow in popularity through the 1950s. Some momentum was lost in the '60s, as potential new members had other things on their minds besides reading the books their parents admired, but the organization endured and continues to this day.

Our local library hosts a Great Books group that meets every other Friday at noon. Its discussion leader, Irving Sanders, has been leading the group for the last seventeen years.

"I'm a graduate of the University of Chicago and knew Mortimer Adler personally and President Hutchins, too," he told me. He received his bachelor's and master's degrees in social service administration from Chicago and worked as a mental health administrator for many years. The Great Books group has always been a hobby.

Irving began leading Great Books discussions thirty-five years ago, when he and his wife lived in Newton, Massachusetts. Then they moved to Miami Beach, where he led a group for fifteen years before moving the hour north to Delray Beach.

Who typically joins Great Books groups? "I've had very fine people in all the groups—professionals, statisticians, folks who worked at the State Department in foreign service—an equal number of men and women," Irving told me. "In Newton we had a member who was chair of the classics department at Wellesley College and a number of scientists—a mathematician and a physicist."

But there is no prerequisite of any educational background, Irving hastened to add. "We've had very good people who had limited formal education but have done a lot of reading all their lives."

The program follows what the foundation calls the Shared Inquiry Method, in which a group leader such as Irving asks questions that have no correct answers and leads discussions rather than providing a lecture. No secondary sources such as book reviews or literary criticisms are allowed. Everyone reads the same copy of the books and sticks to the texts.

What are some of the favorite classics? "Everybody likes *Hamlet*," Irving said. "It's Shakespeare's greatest tragedy and probably his greatest play. Shakespeare isn't the easiest reading, either," he added.

When asked how many times he has read *Hamlet*, Irving replied, "I can't count. In high school and college, and I've led it in six or seven groups—three times with this group." Is it different each time? "Oh sure, that's why they are Great Books; they can be read and re-read many times. It's different each time because the people are different. The people are wonderful."

I asked Irving who would most likely enjoy membership in a Great Books group. "I would say they should like to read and discuss what they read. These are the great ideas of the Western world. We deal with the major issues, for which there are no yes-or-no answers."

As for which books he liked best, "That's like asking a parent which of your children you like best," he joked. "I'm very fond of Plato and Aristotle, and the Greek dramatists, Aeschylus, Sophocles—he's one of my favorites. You've got to have some Greeks, and always a selection from the Bible. I alternate between the Old and the New Testament. One of my favorites is Matthew. Everybody knows some of the things in Matthew, but they don't know where they came from, such as feeding the fishes."

Mark Cwik, a man in his forties who does cabinetry work during the day, leads a Great Books group that meets in a bookstore on Michigan Avenue in Chicago. He's been leading the group for seven years and has also worked on the staff of the Great Books Foundation, which is still based in Chicago.

Mark described the makeup of a typical Great Books group. "They resemble the audience for traditional cultural activities, like the theater and symphony. A good portion of our membership has been in our group a long, long time. I know of several who started in 1947 or '49 and have been in that many years—it's a lifelong passion.

"Solitary reading often is not enough to get it," said Mark. "And that's why the Great Books groups were invented."

Some practical advice

It's often difficult to find private book groups and, when you do, to join them. Many groups don't add members until someone leaves, which is seldom. Some actually have waiting lists. Also, it can be uncomfortable trying out a private group. If it's not a match, there may be feelings of rejection on both sides.

Public groups are easier to find and try out at libraries and bookstores. Guests are more frequent, and often there will be a list of the group's reading for the next six or twelve months. And if you like a wide variety of members, a public group is more likely to give it to you.

It's important to find a group that fits your schedule. One woman who worked regular hours joined a group of women who did not work outside the home and who met midday.

She came late, left early, and lasted only four months.

For audiobook lovers, the ability to read with their ears rather than their eyes can make the difference. Dee Moustakas's group will select only books that are available unabridged on audio in order to accommodate members who otherwise would not be able to participate.

The level of reading and discussion is also, of course, a key factor. One woman I interviewed left her group because it was too serious for her. She wanted more simple enjoyment from her books.

And the leader or facilitator matters greatly. Some groups rotate discussion leaders. Others hire leaders who can vary in their style—from authoritative educators to those who see themselves as facilitators.

Rachel Jacobsohn adopts a facilitator role. "You're going to hear conflicting ideas. One person's insight is no more or less valid than another person's if it can be supported from the text. I like people to get to their own 'aha'."

Personal growth in a group

There are many more types of reading groups, including online groups and mass media groups. The shining star was the one that the talk show host Oprah Winfrey created among her television audience. In addition, with the "One Book, One Community" program that librarian Nancy Pearl created, entire cities across America have now organized themselves to read a book together in the hopes of engendering widespread discussions. It now has offshoots for young readers and their families. More than one type of group activity may appeal to you and yield dividends for your reading life.

Whether to participate in a book group raises the age-old pros and cons of group involvement. You give up a bit of your personal freedom in exchange for the insights that can be gained from discussion. To the extent that you read to expand your knowledge of the world and people, group participation may be well worth the trade-off. The legendary reader Samuel Johnson said, "Books without the knowledge of life are useless, for what should books teach but the art of living?"

Just as exercise classes can push you beyond your normal range of exertion, reading groups can push you beyond your normal insights.

I asked Rachel Jacobsohn what it has meant to her personally to have read so many books and to have led so many discussions. "Reading confirms your aliveness," she said. "It's very validating. That's what book groups ultimately are; you get validated in the human condition—the conditions and puzzles, the good stuff and bad stuff, the aspirations and hopes and despairs. You're not alone out there."

The more I listened to book group members, the more impressed I became. Gradually, admiration turned to envy. My initial skepticism about groups changed to a desire to have that group experience for myself.

I recalled that a group of Chicago businessmen had formed a book club in the 1940s called the Fat Men's Great Books Course (the members were all on the board of the Great Books Foundation). So, with some of my buddies, I started a group that meets every other month at five in the evening at a local pub. We call ourselves the World of Mules Book Group (with thanks to Ogden Nash).

I'm smiling as I write this, happy to be reading together as friends. Happy for the fellowship.

What counts, in the long run, is not what you read; it is what you sift through your own mind; it is the ideas and impressions that are aroused in you by your reading.

—Eleanor Roosevelt

5

A Life Uplifted

As I was writing this chapter, I happened to be in Florence for a week of meetings combined with museum visits. Seeing the art in the Uffizi Gallery and elsewhere, and having books on my mind, I was struck by how often books were included in Renaissance paintings and sculpture.

The forgotten divinity of books

Books seemed to appear everywhere, often dressed in fine leather with elaborate buckles. In one painting, a figure closes a book lightly on her fingers while she looks off, as if transfixed in thought. One sculpture in Santa Maria del Fiore Cathedral shows an angel offering an inkpot to a man dipping his quill, poised to write in a book. Renaissance art is replete with such symbols, including, most famously, Michelangelo's Sistine Chapel.

Most of the books are meant to symbolize Scripture. But they are shown with such loving reverence, it's almost as if the artists were depicting the books themselves as divine objects.

One need not be of any religious persuasion to be awed by what books can do for a person, a culture, and a civilization. In Renaissance times few people could read; books were made by hand and were rare and valuable. It was also a deeply religious age, so it's understandable that people assigned religious symbolism to books. Today, books are so plentiful and inexpensive, we take them for granted. And not just books, but reading, too.

When life is too good

One of the challenges that many of us face when wishing to bring more books into our life is that life is too good. All the enticements, pleasures, and engaging commitments that fill our lives can distract us from a full life of the mind. Sometimes when life isn't so good, the quiet solace of books comes to the rescue. And it can deliver a life even richer than the one we were happy to live before.

It was while suffering through a failing marriage (a second one at that), in that stressful period of self-doubt and worry about children, that a friend of mine got into reading in a big way. He read history, biography, and the pure escape of espionage. Nothing, he told me, could take him away like a book. Now remarried and at a much happier point in his life, he avidly collects new titles, talks books, recommends books, and reads with a passion. For all the pain of his divorce, he is thankful for his union with books.

For another friend, it was his old high school football injury that led to an epiphany. While in his early thirties, his back pain became so debilitating that he had to spend nine months in bed before and after surgery. It was during that time—well after college and graduate school—that he finally fell in love with books and remains so to this day.

For the famed art historian Bernard Berenson, it was while in hiding from the Nazis and Fascists during World War II that reading became his sanctuary. Together with his wife and their assistant, the three hid in the Italian countryside amid their great private library. Their forced seclusion proved to be a blessing for their minds. Berenson, then seventy-seven, kept a diary on his reading and re-reading that was published in 1942 as *One Year's Reading for Fun.*

For others, it was prison that led to enlightenment. In *The Autobiography of Malcolm X*, we learn how Malcolm Little found his salvation in a magnificent library that a man named Parkhurst donated to the prison colony in Norfolk, Massachusetts, where he was incarcerated. Reading freed him.

> *Anyone who has read a great deal can imagine the new world that opened. Let me tell you something: from then until I left that prison, in every free moment I had, if I was not reading in the library, I was reading on my bunk. You couldn't have gotten me out of books with a wedge....months passed without my even thinking about being imprisoned. In fact, up to then, I never had been so truly free in my life....the ability to read awoke inside me some long dormant craving to be mentally alive.*

Nelson Mandela, the first black president of South Africa, was already a university graduate and a practicing attorney when he began what would be a twenty-six-and-a-half-year prison term. "Little can be said in favor of prison, but enforced isolation is conducive to study," he wrote in his autobiography, *Long Walk to Freedom*. In prison, Mandela created his own Great Books study program.

> *I had read some of the classic Greek plays...and found them enormously elevating. What I took out of them was*

*that character was measured by facing up to difficult
situations and that a hero was a man who would not
break even under the most trying circumstances.*

For the novelist Louis L'Amour, it was growing up poor and
being deprived of a formal education that gave him a thirst to
learn. He found it first in those cheap Little Blue Books of classics
abundant in the 1920s, and that hobos traded to while away the
time. They turned to gold in his hands.

The scholar and columnist Thomas Sowell was also raised in a
poor environment. As a youngster, new to New York, his friend Eddie
took him to this curious and dazzling place called the public library.

*Impressed but puzzled as to why we were in a building
with so many books, when I had no money to buy books,
I found it all difficult to understand at first, as Eddie
patiently explained to me how a public library worked.
Unknown to me at the time, it was a turning point in
my life, for I then developed the habit of reading books.*

You don't have to be poor, heartbroken, sick, or imprisoned to
see the light of books. You can be wise enough to understand their
power and live your well-read life when life is good; it's just harder.
In our land of opportunities and distractions, it's hard to devote
our attention to the quiet pleasures of reading. It's as if we live our
lives in a noisy restaurant and can't have the intimate conversation
we most yearn for.

We know it is human nature to take for granted what is plentiful. So we take books for granted; we take the paper they are

printed on for granted; we even take reading glasses for granted. In *The Book*, the historian Barbara Tuchman points out that both paper and reading glasses were invented in the thirteenth century. "When one stops to consider what life would be like without the ability to read after age forty or thereabouts, and the consequences for the life of the mind in general, eyeglasses suddenly appear as important as the wheel."

On being a nonconformist

"Whoso would be a man, must be a nonconformist." When expanded to include women, Emerson's message from his 1841 essay "Self-Reliance" still holds today. Being your own person means being your own reader and caring not what you're *supposed* to read or like. "The greatest thing in the world is to know how to be one's own self," observed Montaigne. Reading according to your own plan is an essential part of learning how to be one's own self.

"What counts, in the long run," said Eleanor Roosevelt, "is not what you read; it is what you sift through your own mind; it is the ideas and impressions that are aroused in you by your reading."

Your Living Library, and how you use it, has more possibilities than your DNA. Only four building blocks make up your DNA; by contrast, think of the number of books that can join you in your library. Imagine all their words and meanings. Even if another person selected the exact same books, that person would not read them in the same way, nor derive the same meanings, ideas, and feelings from them as you. The more you experience and the more you get from your books, the more you will express your individuality.

A story is told that during his stay in Paris, Benjamin Franklin was asked what he considered a man's most pitiable condition. "A lonesome man on a rainy day who does not know how to read," he replied.

Today we have more news and entertainment available than ever before. We don't have to be lonely on a rainy day. But do these make up for books? Mass media, Barbara Tuchman points out, tend toward mass audiences in order to make the economics of production and advertising work. Books, by virtue of their plenitude and heterogeneity, can never represent a mass culture, she says, and thus, "the book remains the carrier of civilization, the voice of the individual."

A life of reading—or not

A children's librarian once shared with me a common refrain among her colleagues: "All it takes is one book." They mean it takes only one book to spark a child's interest in reading that can continue for a lifetime. The same concept can apply to an adult who is ready to be reborn to a life of reading. All it takes is one book to renew your well-read life. Max Perkins, the famed Scribner's editor, would encourage his authors with the reminder that nothing was as important as a book could be. And in *Walden*, Thoreau tells us: "How many a man has dated a new era in his life from the reading of a book."

But if we don't work to improve our own abilities in reading, our talents can wither.

In his later years, Sir Robert Walpole, England's prime minister in the mid-eighteenth century, was said to have had this unsettling experience:

After his arduous years in office, Walpole looked forward to
retirement in his splendid mansion, Houghton Castle.
Entering the library, he took down a book, perused it for a
few minutes, and then returned it to the shelf. He took
down another, but held that only half as long before
replacing it and taking a third. This he immediately put
back, and, bursting into tears, exclaimed, "I have led a life
of business so long that I have lost my taste for reading,
and now—what shall I do?"

Contrast this unhappy fate with Cicero's fate seventeen centuries earlier. Cicero wrote that the reading of literature and the study of science can involve one in useful and amusing study one's whole life long. "No condition can be imagined more happy than such calm enjoyments, in the leisure and quiet of old age." Today we call Cicero's happy enjoyments lifelong learning.

Alone together

One of the obstacles people face when trying to find more time to read is that somehow it seems strange to sit with your partner in the same room and read your separate books. Many people feel they have to watch television or a movie to avoid being social misfits. Yet others manage to slip this conventional view.

A friend of mine who raised a couple of wonderful, high-achieving sons explained how he read to them at night, as so many parents have done, and then went a step further. When they got older and wanted to read their own books, he would still come to their bedroom at night to read his own. He said, "I wanted them to be comfortable with the idea that people can read and be together at the same time."

I came across the same practice when I visited Alexandra Stoddard and her husband, Peter Brown. Both of them are people of great accomplishment: authors, speakers, and hungry readers. As we sat in their beautifully decorated Manhattan apartment and sipped our drinks, we talked about the books we'd been reading, theirs on the coffee table with freshly planted bookmarks. Alexandra explained how much they relished reading their books in their flower-filled living room. "Peter and I have spent thirty-plus delicious years reading together quietly and peacefully, and sharing thoughts in between books. We call it being alone together."

Finally...reading deliberately

To live fully your well-read life—at any age—it is essential to take your selection of books seriously. When you drift from book to book, you are lulled into thinking that this lack of focus is right and natural—but it's as wrong as can be. Some serendipity in your reading is delightful, but if you wanted to build a house, would you wait for the materials to assemble themselves?

And who wouldn't want to know one's inner self better—to discover your talents and develop them further? Yet do we really listen to ourselves long enough to inventory our interests and take advantage of our reading to help us explore and develop those interests?

Taking charge of your reading life means seeking out the best books for you, then buying all you can to have them in your ever-expanding Library of Candidates. If you can't buy all you'd like to, write down their titles in your List of Candidates. Borrow from the library or buy them when you can.

Collecting titles and the actual books that complement your interests is essential preparation. Whether it's Beaujolais or business principles, orcas or orchids, seeking out the best books ever written on your subjects holds the keys to your kingdoms. Ask people who ought to know for their recommendations, and about the books that are available. It's really that simple, yet few people pursue their reading choices deliberately, let alone avidly, in this manner. You will find that one book leads to another and another, like magical stepping stones throughout your life.

Allow plenty of shelf space for your Library of Candidates. As these books accumulate, you may want to dedicate different sections to your current interests. Remember to have a shelf for books that don't fit any category, too. And give yourself the gift of empty shelves. Like an open road, they hold the promise of your future examined life.

It's okay not to take it all seriously

Having taken your reading list *more* seriously, you might take other things about reading *less* seriously—starting with those famous classics.

Sure, examine lists of prize-winning books, important books, bestsellers, Great Works of the Western World, or whatever world you're interested in. Other people have found these books exemplary. You may, too. Don't reject them just *because* they are renowned or popular, but don't accept them for that, either.

Learned people disagree strenuously over art, history, science, and nearly everything else that is written about. Over the years tastes change, often dramatically. Books thought indispensable in one generation are forgotten in the next. And most likely, one book published this year is destined to appear on a list of "Greatest Books of the Twenty-First Century," but won't be recognized as such for another twenty years. Perhaps you will discover that book before the world does.

There is nothing for it but to develop your own list of classics. Remember, the goal is not the list but the *making* of the list. Clifton Fadiman came up with his list of best books, his "lifetime reading plan," and bless his heart for doing so. But no one has, or will, benefit from his list as much as Fadiman himself. Coming up with his list was a fulfilling labor of love for him, just as coming up with your list can be for you.

As for the critics and others who vie for the high ground of literary judgment, listen to them if you find their commentary interesting, but don't take their pronouncements too seriously. Trust your own instincts when reading book reviews as well as books. Feel free to skip over introductions written by someone other than the author; they will often mean more if you read them after you have finished the actual work.

I also hope you take less seriously the need to finish books you've started. Despite your doing a good job of selecting promising candidates, not all these books will be worth finishing. Some just won't speak to you. When that happens, no matter how highly touted the books may be, give up. Too many superb books—superb by *your* standard—are awaiting your attention. And you are fated, like everyone else, not to discover even a fraction of them. Does a sommelier drink down every wine he tastes? If you are not setting some books aside unfinished, you are not sampling enough books.

And I hope you remember that the conventional view of a well-read life—that at some point you will suddenly be well-read—is a mirage. People may label you a well-read person, but it's a hollow honor. Many of those who have read the most are the most humble about it. They know enough to know the breathtaking gaps in their own knowledge.

A few last points I hope you do take seriously

Do take seriously the seemingly innocent question: "Are you reading something great right now?" By choosing your books well and having shelves full of enticing candidates, you'll ensure that you always can be reading a great book. I fervently wish that for you.

I also hope that when you read to learn, you take your time seriously. That is, I hope you read actively, asking yourself questions you expect the book to answer, and take notes. Much is contained in Emerson's line, "There is creative reading as well as creative writing."

If you haven't done so, I encourage you to at least try writing passionately in your books. See if it doesn't help you gain even more from the author and yourself. If, however, you just can't bring yourself to leave footprints, I respect that. As a Preservationist, you will pass on gifts to future readers who may someday treasure your unmarked books.

And I hope you don't close a good book for good when you first finish it. Open it the next day and review what you just learned, even if there seems no need to do so. The fruits of memory grow in your brain the way a tree grows from daily watering, even before it seems to need water. Pick up your finished book a few more times, at longer intervals, and your miraculous mind will retain those particular fruits of memory ever after. Store these books in your Living Library where they can keep you company. "A good book is never exhausted. It goes on whispering to you from the wall," said Anatole Broyard. Buy hardcovers and use them as slim filing containers. Make them trusty working tools. Give away copies of your favorite books and you will gain from them even more.

As an attorney practices law or a physician medicine, think of yourself as practicing reading. Expect to continuously improve and you will.

If you have not taken audiobooks seriously, I hope you will. Still viewed with prejudice by many educated people as not real reading, audiobooks will, in time, achieve the respect they deserve as a new art form, with a heritage even more venerable than that of printed books. Listening compared with silent reading has advantages and disadvantages, but the books you take in are no less—and are sometimes more—in the listening. Don't miss this wondrous way to bring more books into your life.

Also take seriously the practice of reading aloud. Read to children who already know how to read. Read to your partner. Read to other adults. We humans are built for hearing words and are shaped by it. Reading silently to yourself is like being touched; being read to is like being caressed. It's one of the things human beings thrive on.

And seriously consider joining, or starting, a book group. Reading in solitude is lovely indeed, yet we benefit also by fellowship.

In *Fiddler on the Roof*, when Tevye sings "If I Were a Rich Man," he crowns his dream of rooms by the dozen and a yard full of geese with: "And I'd discuss the holy books with the learned men.../This would be the sweetest thing of all." What better experience to purchase with a bit of our earnings than the time to talk with our fellow readers about books, ideas, and the meaning of life?

Take seriously the list you keep of what books you've read and when you read them. Better yet, make notes on what the book meant to you. It's a rare person who doesn't wish for such a list, yet it's an even rarer person who keeps one. Record your Bookography and see if, like a friend, it becomes a cherished gift you give yourself.

Lasting book love

On the first page of this little guide, I suggested that I could help you find more time to read. I hope that by employing some of the ideas in this little book and others you discover, you'll fall deeply in book love—not just once but perpetually. Then you will not have to worry about finding the time to read; that time will come to you. You will naturally do some things less as you read more. What those things will be is obviously your decision.

Finally, I hope you read some books for no reason other than pure enjoyment. Let a fine story grab hold of you, let yourself be embraced in this uniquely human pleasure with sweet abandon. As you collect books for learning, also collect books that make you laugh and cry and shudder and forget the real world completely. It is good for us in more ways than we know.

Epilogue

The experience of writing this book has been uplifting and humbling, for I have learned enough to understand the magnitude of the subject matter and the mere baby steps I've taken in its treatment. I hope that this little guide will help lead you to the life-changing books that await your open mind and heart.

On your journey, if you discover new ways to live your well-read life that you think might help others, I would consider it a favor if you would share your ideas with me so that I can continue to improve on this effort.

You are welcome to write me at either Levenger, Well-Read Life, 420 South Congress Avenue, Delray Beach, Florida 33445 or wellreadlife@levenger.com.

My wish for you, dear reader, is that you find all that you imagine to be waiting for you within the world of books. I wish this kind of book love for you—and lots of it.

Whatever you can do, or dream you can, begin it.
Boldness has genius, power and magic in it.

—Goethe

Bibliography

Adler, Mortimer J., and Charles Van Doren. *How to Read a Book: The Classic Guide to Intelligent Reading.* Rev. ed. New York: Simon & Schuster, Touchstone, 1972.

Agardy, Franklin J. *How to Read Faster and Better: How to Get Everything You Want from Anything You Read as Fast as You Can Think.* New York: Simon & Schuster, 1981.

Alter, Robert. *The Pleasures of Reading in an Ideological Age.* New York: Simon & Schuster, 1989.

Armstrong, William H. *Study Is Hard Work.* 2nd ed. Jaffrey, N.H.: David R. Godine, 2002.

Atkinson, Brooks, ed. *The Selected Writings of Ralph Waldo Emerson.* New York: Random House, 1992.

Baldwin, James. *The Book-Lover: A Guide to the Best Reading.* Chicago: Jansen, McClurg, 1885.

Battles, Matthew. *Library: An Unquiet History.* New York: W. W. Norton, 2003.

Beamon, Bob, and Milana Walter Beamon. *The Man Who Could Fly: The Bob Beamon Story.* Columbus, Miss.: Genesis Press, 1999.

Berenson, Bernard. *One Year's Reading for Fun.* New York: Alfred A. Knopf, 1960.

Berg, A. Scott. *Max Perkins: Editor of Genius.* New York: E. P. Dutton, 1978.

Bernard, André. *Rotten Reflections: A Literary Companion.* New York: Pushcart Press, 1990.

Bettmann, Otto L. *Bettmann: The Picture Man.* Ed. Norman Sheffield Jr. Gainesville, Fla.: Board of Regents of the State of Florida, 1992.

———. *The Delights of Reading: Quotes, Notes & Anecdotes.* Boston: David R. Godine, 1987.

Birkerts, Sven. *The Gutenberg Elegies: The Fate of Reading in an Electronic Age.* Boston and London: Faber and Faber, 1994.

Bloom, Harold. *How to Read and Why.* New York: Scribner, 2000.

Brown, Helen Gurley. *I'm Wild Again: Snippets from My Life and a Few Brazen Thoughts.* New York: St. Martin's Press, 2000.

Calvino, Italo. *Why Read the Classics?* Trans. Martin McLaughlin. New York: Random House, Pantheon, 1999.

Carroll, Lewis. *Feeding the Mind.* Delray Beach, Fla.: Levenger Press, 1999.

Cerf, Bennett. *At Random: The Reminiscences of Bennett Cerf.* New York: Random House, 1977.

Churchill, Winston S. *Painting as a Pastime.* Delray Beach, Fla.: Levenger Press, 2002.

Delbanco, Andrew. *Required Reading: Why Our American Classics Matter Now.* New York: Farrar, Straus and Giroux, 1997.

Denby, David. *Great Books: My Adventures with Homer, Rousseau, Woolf, and Other Indestructible Writers of the Western World.* New York: Simon & Schuster, 1996.

Dimnet, Ernest. *The Art of Thinking.* New York: Simon and Schuster, 1942.

Donaldson, Gerald. *Books.* Oxford: Phaidon Press, 1981.

Douglass, Frederick. *Narrative of the Life of an American Slave.* New Brunswick, N.J.: Transaction Publishers, 1998.

Dushkin, David A. *Psychology Today: An Introduction.* Del Mar, Calif.: CRM Inc., 1970.

Epstein, Jason. *Book Business: Publishing Past Present and Future.* New York: W. W. Norton, 2001.

Fadiman, Anne. *Ex Libris: Confessions of a Common Reader.* New York: Farrar, Straus and Giroux, 1998.

Fadiman, Clifton. *The Lifetime Reading Plan.* Cleveland: World Publishing, 1960.

———. *The Little, Brown Book of Anecdotes.* 3rd ed. Boston: Little, Brown, 1985.

Gilbar, Steven, ed. *Reading in Bed: Personal Essays on the Glories of Reading.* Lincoln, Mass.: David R. Godine, 1995.

Gill, Brendan. *Late Bloomers.* New York: Artisan, 1996.

Gingerich, Owen. *The Book Nobody Read: Chasing the Revolutions of Nicolaus Copernicus.* New York: Walker & Company, 2004.

Glaspey, Terry W. *A Passion for Books.* Eugene, Ore.: Harvest House, 1998.

Hamilton, John Maxwell. *Casanova Was a Book Lover: And Other Naked Truths and Provocative Curiosities About the Writing, Selling and Reading of Books.* Baton Rouge: Louisiana State University Press, 2000.

Henderson, Bill. *Rotten Reviews: A Literary Companion.* Stamford, Conn.: Pushcart Press, 1986.

———. *Rotten Reviews II: A Literary Companion.* Stamford, Conn.: Pushcart Press, 1987.

Jackson, Holbrook. *The Reading of Books*. New York: Scribner's, 1947.

Jacobsohn, Rachel W. *The Reading Group Handbook: Everything You Need to Know from Choosing Members to Leading Discussions*. New York: Hyperion, 1994.

Korda, Michael. *Another Life: A Memoir of Other People*. New York: Random House, 1999.

———. *Making the List: A Cultural History of the American Bestseller, 1900–1999*. New York: Barnes & Noble Books, 2001.

L'Amour, Louis. *Education of a Wandering Man: A Memoir*. New York: Bantam Books, 1989.

Laskin, David, and Holly Hughes. *The Reading Group Book: The Complete Guide to Starting and Sustaining a Reading Group, with Annotated Lists of 250 Titles for Provocative Discussion*. New York: Penguin Group, 1995.

Lewis, Norman. *How to Read Better and Faster*. New York: Thomas Y. Crowell, 1962.

MacDonald, John D. *Reading for Survival*. Washington, D.C.: Library of Congress, 1987.

MacLean, Malcolm S., and Elizabeth K. Holmes, eds. *Men and Books*. New York: Richard R. Smith, 1932.

Mandela, Nelson. *Long Walk to Freedom: The Autobiography of Nelson Mandela*. New York: Little, Brown, 1994.

Manguel, Alberto. *A History of Reading*. New York: Penguin Group, 1996.

McCullough, David. *John Adams*. New York: Simon & Schuster, 2001.

Mencken, H. L. *Happy Days 1880-1892*. New York: Alfred A. Knopf, 1963.

Miller, Henry. *The Books in My Life*. New York: New Directions, 1969.

Moorehead, Alan. *Darwin and the Beagle*. New York: Harper & Row, 1969.

Nelson, Sara. *So Many Books, So Little Time: A Year of Passionate Reading*. New York: G.P. Putnam's Sons, 2003.

Osen, Diane, ed. *The Book That Changed My Life*. New York: National Book Foundation, 2002.

Pauk, Walter. *How to Study in College*. 7th ed. Boston: Houghton Mifflin, 2001.

Pearl, Nancy. *Book Lust: Recommended Reading for Every Mood, Moment, and Reason*. Seattle: Sasquatch Books, 2003.

Pearlman, Mickey. *What to Read: The Essential Guide for Reading Group Members and Other Book Lovers.* New York: HarperCollins, 1994.

Pennac, Daniel. *Better Than Life.* Trans. David Homel. Toronto: Coach House Press, 1992.

Pitkin, Walter B. *The Art of Rapid Reading.* New York: McGraw-Hill, 1929.

Quindlen, Anna. *How Reading Changed My Life.* New York: Ballantine Books, 1998.

Robinson, Francis P. *Effective Study.* Rev. ed. New York: Harper & Row, 1961.

Roosevelt, Eleanor. *You Learn by Living.* New York: Harper & Brothers, 1960.

Saal, Rollene. *The New York Public Library Guide to Reading Groups.* New York: Crown, 1995.

Sabine, Gordon, and Patricia Sabine. *Books That Made the Difference: What People Told Us.* (Abridged.) N.p.: Book-of-the-Month Club, 1984.

Sample, Steven B. *The Contrarian's Guide to Leadership.* San Francisco: Jossey-Bass, 2002.

Sandburg, Carl. *Harvest Poems, 1910–1960.* New York: Harcourt, Brace & World, 1960.

Sanders, Tim. *Love Is the Killer App: How to Win Business and Influence Friends.* New York: Crown Business, 2002.

Saricks, Joyce G., and Nancy Brown. *Readers' Advisory Service in the Public Library.* 2nd ed. Chicago and London: American Library Association, 1997.

Shearer, Kenneth D., and Robert Burgin, eds. *The Readers' Advisor's Companion.* Englewood, Colo.: Greenwood Publishing Group, 2001.

Singh, Simon. *Fermat's Enigma: The Epic Quest to Solve the World's Greatest Mathematical Problem.* New York: Walker and Company, 1997.

Slezak, Ellen, ed. *The Book Group Book: A Thoughtful Guide to Forming and Enjoying a Stimulating Book Discussion Group.* Chicago: Chicago Review Press, 2000.

Slights, William W. *Managing Readers: Printed Marginalia in English Renaissance Books.* Ann Arbor: University of Michigan Press, 2001.

Sowell, Thomas. *A Personal Odyssey.* New York: Simon & Schuster, The Free Press, 2000.

Stoddard, Alexandra. *Choosing Happiness: Keys to a Joyful Life.* New York: HarperCollins, 2002.

Szekely, Edmond Bordeaux. *The Art of Study: The Sorbonne Method.* N.p.: International Biogenic Society, 1991.

Targ, William, ed. *Carrousel for Bibliophiles: A Treasury of Tales, Narratives, Songs, Epigrams and Sundry Curious Studies Relating to a Noble Theme.* New York: Duschnes Crawford, 1947.

Tides of War: Recording the Audio Version. New York: C-SPAN Recorded Books, 2000.

Tuchman, Barbara W. *The Book.* Washington, D.C.: Library of Congress, 1980.

Unger, Harlow Giles. *Noah Webster: The Life and Times of an American Patriot.* New York: John Wiley & Sons, 1998.

Vance, Mike, and Diane Deacon. *Think Out of the Box.* Franklin Lakes, N.J.: Career Press, 1995.

Warren, Dale, ed. *What Is a Book? Thoughts About Writing.* Boston: Houghton Mifflin, 1935.

Weber, J. Sherwood, ed. *Good Reading: A Helpful Guide for Serious Readers.* Rev. ed. New York: New American Library, 1964.

Woolf, Virginia. *The Common Reader, Second Series.* London: Hogarth Press, 1932.

X, Malcolm. *Autobiography.* 2nd ed. Epilogue by Alex Haley. New York: Ballantine Books, 1999.

Young, James Webb. *A Technique for Producing Ideas.* Chicago: NTC/Contemporary Publishing, 1975.

Zinsser, William. *American Places: A Writer's Pilgrimage to 16 of This Country's Most Visited and Cherished Sites.* New York: Akadine Press, 2002.

Acknowledgments

My first thanks go to those readers who shared with me their thirst for more time to read. They made me curious about whether time might actually be found. Because of them, I sought the guidance of many hundreds of accomplished readers, both living and through history. I've mentioned many of these people in the text and bibliography, and I am grateful to each of them.

An even greater number of readers are not mentioned in the text but have helped by patiently answering my questions. Beyond the formal interviews, many have helped me informally because for years it seems I have been unable to have an ordinary conversation. Like some tenacious reporter, I keep asking nearly everyone I meet, "So, are you reading a good book?" in the hopes of snaring them into a lengthy oral Bookography. There is no way to acknowledge all the kind people who responded. For some, like my cab drivers, I never got their names. So to all who talked with me in recent years about reading, my humble thanks.

A couple of subjects covered in the book merit special mention. For my understanding of speed reading, I am indebted to Robert Blecha, John Harrison, and Helene Selco. For the history of the Great Books Foundation I thank Steven Craig, Peter Lamar, and George Schueppert.

To understand reading groups, it helped to have one of my own, and for this I thank the members of our World of Mules Book Group not otherwise mentioned, including Amir Abtahi, Jeff Parker, Gary Spielfolgel, Lawrence Steinberg, Michael Tiernan, John Ury, and Wayne Welch.

Writers, editors, and librarians are professional readers, and I was blessed to have had the knowing assistance of many of them, including Mykal G. Banta, Stewart Brand, David Brown, Andrew Carroll, Andre Dubus III, Benjamin A. Eason, Ken Esrig, Mark Ford, George Gibson,

ACKNOWLEDGMENTS

Karen Granger, Robert Greenman, Ted Hartley, Roger Hurlburt, P. D. James, Mike Kami, Marzi Kaplan, Kevin Kelly, Lawrence Kutner, Irving R. Levine, Hershel Gordon Lewis, Scott Matthews, John D. Miller, Eugene Miller, Jeff Perlman, Luke Pontifell, Will Provine, Laura Roberts, Jeffrey Seglin, Dava Sobel, and Nanette Wiser.

In addition to the librarians already noted, other beloved keepers of the book include Lee LaFleur at Cornell University, John J. Callahan III, Kathleen M. Hensman and Kristin A. Reinke at the Delray Beach Public Library, William Miller at Florida Atlantic University, Jean Trebbi at the Florida Center for the Book, and Joseph J. Bray and Brian Schottlaender at the University of California, San Diego.

Of the many booksellers who came to my assistance, I would like to particularly thank Martin Manley, Mark Nason, and Christine Putman of Alibris; Avin Mark Domnitz of the American Booksellers Association; Mitchell Kaplan of Books & Books; and Gregory P. Josefowicz of Borders.

Many serious readers suggested helpful books or provided feedback on this one, and I am indebted to them all. Among them: Tony Altmann, Mike Arents, Lester M. Bradshaw, John Brook, Kenneth Brook, Tami Brook, Cheryl Budd, John Burke, Dave Corey, Frank Curtis, Surabhi Desai, Niels Diffrient, James Donnelly, Doris Elkin, Douglas Fitzgerald, Carlo Franzblau, James C. Fuscoe III, Jacqueline Gerbus, Robert Giampietro, Richard E. Goldman, Bill Henry, George Ittner, Ming Ivory, John Jaquette, Tina Kislak, Steve Klingel, Darlene Kostrub, Nancy Lee, Brad Lucas, Marty Miller, Tom Morris, Asuka Nakahara, Kenneth Nisch, Richard G. Overman, Deborah Pearce, Terry Pfeil, Michael Platner, Gene Pokorny, Mary Rodriguez, Wills Ryan, Jerry Shereshewsky, Bill Tahnk, Andrea Weiss, Kim Wheeler, Kenny Young, and Bob Zobel.

ACKNOWLEDGMENTS

I thank all two thousand readers who took part in Levenger's online conversation about writing in books, and particularly those I quoted: Linda Bermingham Addy, Maryjane Ashworth-King, Victoria Caasi-Escuton, Cherie Carter, Joy E. Hensley, Susan Parris, and The Rev. Douglas G. Scott.

Levenger staff members inspire me every workday about our role in serving readers, writers, and thinkers. I would like to thank each of them. And this little guide must seem otherwise to my faithful assistant, who compiled the bibliography, obtained all permissions, and checked out one detail or another on nearly every page. A thousand thanks to you, Sue Olund.

The Levenger Press gang that put together the little-book-that-would-never-finish includes Vicki Ehrenman, Danielle Furci, Lee Passarella, and Jeff Simon—a handful of people with a roomful of talent. Christine Belleris, Luise Erdmann, and Megan Gordon were of great help in bringing the manuscript together.

The heart of Levenger Press is our editor, Mim Harrison. This book would not exist without her. Her gifted editing and constant encouragement kept me going. Against the odds, and to the abiding gratitude of its readers, she kept this little guide little.

Finally, I have learned why writers thank their families. To Lori, Cal, and Corey: you are the living that my reading is for.

Index

Notes

Notes

Notes

Notes

Notes

Notes

Notes

'Read, read, read. Do, do. do.'

—Louis L' Amour

Uncommon Books
for Serious Readers

Boston
Henry Cabot Lodge

Feeding the Mind
Lewis Carroll

A Fortnight in the Wilderness
Alexis de Tocqueville

The Little Guide to Your Well-Read Life
Steve Leveen

New York
Theodore Roosevelt

Painting as a Pastime
Winston S. Churchill

Rare Words
Jan Leighton
and Hallie Leighton

Samuel Johnson's Dictionary
Selections from the 1755 work
that defined the English language
Edited by Jack Lynch

Samuel Johnson's Insults
Edited by Jack Lynch

The Silverado Squatters
Six selected chapters
Robert Louis Stevenson

Sir Winston Churchill's Life Through His Paintings
David Coombs
with Minnie Churchill
Foreword by Mary Soames

Words That Make a Difference
Robert Greenman

Levenger Press is the publishing arm of

LEVENGER
TOOLS FOR SERIOUS READERS

www.Levenger.com   800-544-0880

LEVENGER STORES
Boston   Chicago   Delray Beach